INEXTINGUISHABLE!

By David Mayorga

Edited by Emily Rose King

Table of Contents

(Endorsements

"We don't have to live with a cold heart. Jesus has given us everything we need to burn with love for Him every day. In this book, David lays out practical steps we can take to fiery maintain the fire of our passion for Jesus. Get ready to burn!"

- Bob Sorge, *Author,* Secrets of the Secret Place

"In a time when there are so many distractions and temptations in life, David Mayorga's book reminds us of the necessity to press in to God so we can be refined by the fire of God! David is a good friend, and I've often witnessed his heart of compassion and encouragement. That same heart comes through the pages of this book as encourages us to draw closer to God. May we all fall in love with Jesus all over again and allow Him to refine and purify our hearts!"

- Tom Wilhoit, *Senior Pastor*
Fellowship of Believers Church
Sarasota, Florida

"I have known Pastor David Mayorga for many years and I appreciate his anointing and ministry. His teaching is not for the fainthearted. This is not a message for the soft, comfortable or undedicated believer. These are teachings of breaking, squeezing, digging, seeking, and suffering so the best of God in you comes out. Courage, faith, and trust are what you learn from David's words. May you be blessed and broken!"

- Deborah Hopwood, *Lead Pastor*
Centro Cristiano Oasis de Esperanza
H. Matamoros, Tamaulipas, Mexico

"I've known Pastor Dave Mayorga for over 20 years and every year I see a man more on fire for the Lord than the first day that I've met him. Inextinguishable is more than a book, it is the heart of God through a man of God whose only desire is to be pleasing to God. Inextinguishable will cause you to look at your own life and see if you're fire for the things of God is fresh and still burning, I know I have."

- Tom Carubba, *Senior Pastor*
Hosanna World Changers
Brownsville, Texas

"David Mayorga's latest book, "Inextinguishable!" is must reading for those who need and desire the fire of God in their personal lives. His book gives the follower of Jesus Christ a clear, precise, thought provoking and above all practical approach to this urgent message. This message is not a suggestion, but God's preference! The hymn writer wrote, "Let me burn out for Thee, dear Lord, burn and wear out for Thee."

> - Gerardo Salmerón, *Senior Pastor*
> Iglesia Casa De Oración,
> McAllen, Texas

"Pastor David by the Spirit of God challenges us in this book Inextinguishable! to pause and examine ourselves. It's a big temptation to focus on the externals and neglect your heart condition. When there is a disconnect with the fire you will know. This book to me is the foundation of true personal and corporate revival. Glory to God who has always raised men like David to provoke us to a deeper walk with God. When on fire, we can change the world and that's our mission. We have access to the fire that can change the world."

> - Fred Kasule, *Pastor*
> Go International Foundation,
> Kampala, Uganda, Africa

Foreword

Once again in his latest book INEXTINGUISHABLE! David Mayorga takes us behind the printed Word to the Living Word. One of the lost arts of the average believer is that of meditation.

Someone compared meditation to a cow chewing its cud. The cow first consumes a large amount of grass then lies down and regurgitates it in order to chew it again. This second chewing is similar to the act of meditation.

Too many believers read large portions of the Word but fail to go back and take time to ponder what they have read. The old hymn writer expressed it this way.

Break Thou the Bread of Life,
  Dear Lord, to me,
As Thou didst break the loaves
  Beside the sea;
Beyond the sacred page
  I seek Thee, Lord;
My spirit pants for Thee,
  O Living Word.

The title INEXTINGUISHABLE refers to God Himself as the 'all-consuming fire.'

Fire both fascinates and terrifies, it empowers and purifies, it comforts and consumes, it refines and restricts, it hardens and melts, it attracts and repels, it illuminates and devastates. God reveals Himself to us in many different ways. He desires to consume our fleshly nature, illuminate our understanding, soften our hearts, comfort our souls and fascinates us by His awesome glory.

In this wonderful book, David Mayorga explains how to receive and maintain the fire of God but also how great biblical leaders failed to maintain their fire and thereby lost it.

Finally, INEXTINGUISHABLE focuses on the life of the Apostle Paul and reveals how as a zealous Pharisee he was not able to accomplish anything until he had a personal encounter with the God of fire that totally and radically transformed his life and ministry.
INEXTINGUISHABLE will open up many of these wonderful truths.

It's worth reading but more importantly it's worth meditating on. Like the Apostle Paul you too can experience this transforming fire.

- David Ravenhill, *Author, Itenerant Teacher*
Lakeland, Florida

(Preface

The title of this book is called Inextinguishable. Oxford's Dictionary describes the word like this:

Unable to be extinguished or quenched. i.e. 'a small inextinguishable candle.' Listen to the synonyms: *irrepressible, unquenchable, imperishable, indestructible, undying, unfading, unfailing, unceasing, ceaseless, enduring, lasting, everlasting, eternal, persistent, incessant.*

Picture in your mind a candle or lamp that burns endlessly. It cannot afford to die, so it will not because it cannot!

It is with this heart, that this book has been written. To empower and release those who have never burned for Jesus; to restore those who at one time burned bright for Jesus – but have lost the fire due to various reasons. And to continue fanning the flame on those who are burning passionately for Jesus – the inextinguishable ones!

So, it came to pass…

It was November 26, 2017, while visiting San Antonio, Texas and celebrating my birthday that I awoke early in the morning to thank the Lord for giving me another year of life and to express my worship unto Him, that God visited me in a powerful way.

As I spent time with Jesus in the secret place and thanking Him for my lot in life and the 52 years of precious life He had granted me, I asked the Lord a question: "What does a fifty-two-year-old man look like to You?" Don't ask me why I was asking that, but God knew why, I'm sure. As I waited for the Lord's reply, this is what He showed me:

He showed me a vision of a lamp. The lamp looked a bit old and rustic. It was like those nice antique lamps people buy and place them as décor. I heard a voice say to me, "I know that you are trying to guess how old that lamp is." I said, "Very true Lord." The Lord proceeded to show me the lamp and said, "Does it really matter how old a lamp is? Is the lamp really all that important?" As I sat and wondered the Lord's reply, I saw a hand come from somewhere and it lit the lamp. The lamp then began to burn with such brightness, for the fire in it was bright and intense! After the lamp was burning bright for a while, the Lord said to me, "David, how old do you think the fire is?" "I don't know. You just ignited it, so I guess it's a few minutes old?" I replied. Then the Lord said to me, "David, my fire is an eternal flame. It is always burning. It is always fresh. It is always new. It's not about how valuable the lamp is, but about how fresh the fire is! You can be as fresh and as new as you allow Me to burn within you!" End of my vision.

Here is what I learned from the Lord: It doesn't matter how old or new you think you are; it doesn't matter how big or small you think you might be; and it doesn't matter how other people see you or make you out to be - the only thing that matters is what God thinks of you!

We live and serve a God of the impossible. He will take what you offer Him and then He will multiply it in a million miraculous ways! Father Abraham is a principle example of a burning lamp for God.

After him and his wife Sarai were way over the age of child-bearing, God gave him word that they would bear a son. He would be the son of promise. Listen to the testimony of this burning lamp as it is demonstrated in Romans 4:16-22: **"Therefore it is of faith that it might be according to grace, so that the promise might be sure to all the seed, not only to those who are of the law, but also to those who are of the faith of Abraham, who is the father of us all (as it is written, "I have made you a father of many nations") in the presence of Him whom he believed—God, who gives life to the dead and calls those things which do not exist as though they did; who, contrary to hope, in hope believed, so that he became the father of many nations, according to what was spoken, "So shall your descendants be." And not being weak in faith, he did not consider his own body, already dead (since he was about a hundred years old), and the deadness of Sarah's womb. He did not waver at the promise of God through unbelief, but was strengthened in faith, giving glory to God, and being fully convinced that what He had promised He was also able to perform. And therefore "it was accounted to him for righteousness."**

Abraham **"...did not consider his own body, already dead..."** He never even thought about it twice that he was unable naturally to have children at that age! He simply **"...did not waver at the promise of God through unbelief, but was strengthened in faith..."** This is definitely a Scriptural reference of someone who after many years of walking with God – still burned with faith and desire to see God's promises fulfilled. Apart from the many trials and tests that came upon his life, Abraham remained inextinguishable! Yes, "the lamp" [his body] was old, but not the fire in him. Do you see this?

So, for my birthday, apart from special gifts I received, the Lord also gave me a gift - a vision of a burning lamp and oh yea, the theme to this manuscript, called Inextinguishable!

This vision has set me on a new course of responsibility. Here's my new prayer along with King David's: **"O God, You have taught me from my youth, and hitherto have I declared Your wondrous works. Yes, even when I am old and gray-headed, O God, forsake me not, [but keep me alive] until I have declared Your mighty strength to [this] generation, and Your might and power to all that are to come."** (Psalm 71:17-18 AMP)

By the grace of God, I have made it a point to stay on fire for the rest of my days. This definitely begins with a willful choice and is sustained by a willful choice - my life will be a burning lamp for generations to come for the glory of God. My mind and heart are made up!

In this writing, I have visited many Scriptures, testimonies and practical life experiences to bring about this inextinguishable lifestyle that I am speaking of and teaching on.

My prayer is that once you have read these notes, your life will be also an eternal flame burning for Jesus in a dark and cold world.

- David Mayorga, *Director at Masterbuilder Ministries, Inc.*
  Palmhurst, Texas

PART 1

CREATED
FOR
BURNING!

Chapter 1

First Things First - God Is a Consuming Fire!

"Therefore, since we are receiving a kingdom which cannot be shaken, let us have grace, by which we may serve God acceptably with reverence and godly fear. For our God is a consuming fire." (Hebrews 12:28-29)

When you come and ponder what fire is and what it can potentially do, you will discover that fire is a servant to either do bad or do good. It all depends how you use it. In the natural physical world, we live in, we can see fire as a positive or a negative. You can use fire to cook and prepare a delicious meal, or you can use fire to destroy a whole forest – which won't be a good thing.

In matters of the spiritual world, fire is one of the characteristics of God's nature. The Scripture says that He is a consuming fire.

In the Old Testament when Moses spoke to God's people Israel, He exhorted God's children by saying to them the God is a consuming fire and must be reverenced and feared. Listen to Moses warning God's people regarding the sin of idolatry and what God thought about it: **"Take heed to yourselves, lest you forget the covenant of the Lord your God which He made with you, and make for yourselves a carved image in the form of anything which the Lord your God has forbidden you. For the Lord your God is a consuming fire, a jealous God."** (Deuteronomy 4:23-24)

In the New Testament, the Hebrew writer, also repeats the words of Moses to the disciples of Jesus, saying, **"See that you do not refuse Him who speaks. For if they did not escape who refused Him who spoke on earth, much more shall we not escape if we turn away from Him who speaks from heaven, whose voice then shook the earth; but now He has promised, saying, "Yet once more I shake not only the earth, but also heaven." Now this, "Yet once more," indicates the removal of those things that are being shaken, as of things that are made, that the things which cannot be shaken may remain. Therefore, since we are receiving a kingdom which cannot be shaken, let us have grace, by which we may serve God acceptably with reverence and godly fear. For our God is a consuming fire."** (Hebrews 12:25-29)

As we unfold the subject of fire, we need to understand that God is the same yesterday, today and forever. He is a loving and compassionate God, but He is also a God of order and judgment. He is both. God will not compromise His holiness!

Too often, people feel that God is perpetually angry and wants to destroy everyone; this is what the enemy might want you to think, but it is totally a lie of the devil! God is not angry but is compassionate. He wants to touch your life and restore it to its original purpose. But to do that, He must deal with the sin in our hearts. That is why Jesus came to earth; to live and die at the cross. Through His shed blood, we find remission for sin and acceptance by our loving heavenly Father. It's when the Father hears us pleading the blood of Jesus over our sinful lives, that He forgives and embraces us as His own. This is true adoption. We are adopted into the family of God.

The word "consuming fire" is used to describe God's true nature. He can fill you with His glorious fire of His glory, or He can judge you for your willingness to continue living in sin and corruption. He is a consuming fire!

To further add to God being a consuming fire, the Bible also speaks of God's glory and holiness as a devouring fire. Listen to this in Exodus 24:16, 17 - **"The glory of the Lord abode upon Mount Sinai, and the cloud covered it six days: and the seventh day He called unto Moses out of the midst of the cloud. And the sight of the glory of the Lord was like a devouring fire on the top of the mount in the eyes of the children of Israel."** This part of God's fire would be a positive characteristic.

Now, God's judgment is also described as a consuming fire to destroy the enemies of Israel in the Promised Land. Deuteronomy 9:3 says, **"Understand therefore this day, that the Lord thy God is He which goeth over before thee; as a consuming fire He shall destroy them (Israel's enemies) and He shall bring them down before thy face: so shalt thou drive them out, and destroy them quickly, as the Lord hath said unto thee."**

In His love, God's fire will consume anything that is not part of His holy will for you. He will not tolerate evil and anything that is contrary to His nature. It is His nature to be holy!

Exposed to the Wrath of a Sin Hating God

Every person who has not entered into God's kingdom by the blood of Jesus, remains exposed to the righteous wrath of a God who hates sin with a passion. No wonder some sinners tremble at the thought of God's impending judgment.

It is vital that those who follow God understand that God is a consuming fire. He will either pour out His fire on the believer and make Him glow with His glory, or He will release His fire upon the sinner and judge Him for His continual rejection of God's love and mercy.

The Fire that Purifies

Throughout Scripture, fire also often holds the general idea of purifying or of judgment at various times. Jesus even used the idea of "eternal fire" on two occasions in stories related to judgment upon unbelievers. Look at Matthew 18:8 and also on Matthew 25:41.

The Lord also rained down fire from the sky in judgment upon Sodom and Gomorrah (Genesis 19:24). Fire served as part of offering the sacrifices of the Old Testament. Moses encountered God in a burning bush consumed by fire (Exodus 3). Fire came as a judgment upon the Egyptians (Exodus 9:23-24), yet the Lord also led the people of Israel by fire at night in the wilderness (Exodus 13:22).

If there is anything that I want to solidify in these notes, it is this: God is consuming fire and burns perpetually. It never ends. It is His nature and He will burn for all eternity. He is the Eternal Flame! **"Now I saw heaven opened, and behold, a white horse. And He who sat on him was called Faithful and True, and in righteousness He judges and makes war. His eyes were like a flame of fire, and on His head were many crowns. He had a name written that no one knew except Himself. He was clothed with a robe dipped in blood, and His name is called The Word of God. And the armies in heaven, clothed in fine** linen, white and clean, followed Him on white horses. Now out of His mouth goes a sharp sword, that with it He should strike the nations. And He Himself will rule them with a rod of iron. He Himself treads the winepress of the fierceness and wrath of Almighty God. And He has on His robe and on His thigh a name written: KING OF KINGS AND LORD OF LORDS." (Revelation 19:11–16)

Chapter 2

The Lamp Must Burn Continually!

"Then the Lord spoke to Moses, saying: 'Command the children of Israel that they bring to you pure oil of pressed olives for the light, to make the lamps burn continually. Outside the veil of the Testimony, in the tabernacle of meeting, Aaron shall be in charge of it from evening until morning before the Lord continually; it shall be a statute forever in your generations. He shall be in charge of the lamps on the pure gold lampstand before the Lord continually." (Leviticus 24:1-4)

If there was one particular command God gave Moses, it was this particular one, regarding the lamp inside the tabernacle. The lamp was to be kept burning continually and the Lord gave Moses instructions on how to do this.

When I ponder this Scripture, my mind and heart quickly make their way toward the responsibility the priest had in making sure this lamp never went out. Can you imagine all day, every day, making sure that there was a flame burning?

The seriousness of this lamp burning continually had to be in the forefront of these priest's mind. I have never read of what would actually happen if this lamp stopped burning. It was something that just wouldn't happen. God said, "Keep it burning continually."

And it did!

I have often spoken to Christian believers regarding the fire of God, and how it is needed in our lives and how it makes an impact on others – if it remains burning. The reply usually is the same, "Pastor David, it is not easy keeping the fire burning! There are so many tests and trials we go through and sometimes we get discouraged." Others have said, "I have days when I'm on fire; I also have days when I am cold!"

My friends – the fire of God burning in you, has everything to do with the understanding of the process of upkeep. Let us look deeper into it.

It Begins with the Olives

The future of the lamp's fire begins with the olives. What about the olives? The commandment stated that olives needed to be brought in and pressed, so oil could be collected from them. It was the oil that made it possible for any fire to arise from the lamp. In other words: no olives, no oil; no oil no light!

Olives were brought in to the olive press and there they were pressed. The word pressed comes from the Hebrew word kathith which means beaten. It was through this process that olive oil was collected at least in ancient Nazareth.

As a believer, one must get a real understanding of this process:

The olive is hand-picked. As one goes through the olive trees during the harvesting season (August - November) you will pick them and take them in a basket to the olive press. When God visits our life, whether it be through a direct word from the Lord through a prophet, His Word, or a dream / vision – we can begin to get a sense that God is attempting to do something supernatural in us. We must be attentive to these dealings.

The olive is then pressed. It is in this first pressing, that the olive will be crushed to a paste. After it has been crushed to a paste, it is then taken to another press (a much harder press) – this is when the oil comes forth from the process. The first press is the best oil, the first-fruits. This oil was usually used at the temple for priestly purposes, for example, to light the Menorah. The second pressed oil was used for food, medicine, perfume, and cosmetics. The third and final press was usually used for oil lamps and soap.

It Started with Aaron, Now the Responsibility is Ours!

• Present ourselves as olives to be pressed [beaten].

A life of total surrender. What is a life of total surrender? Well basically, a life of surrender is a life lived with a heart wholly consecrated to God for His use. People who live surrendered lives, are people who have learned to be at God's beck and call. A surrendered vessel of the Lord is the type of individual who won't settle for anything less than pursuing God's heart in all matters.

The yielding of your rights. What constitutes a person's rights? This is one subject many believers today struggle with. To be able to discern what it is that God wants you to keep, and what He needs you to get rid of, usually presents a big problem for many. The secret of knowing what to keep and what to let go of is found in the depth of the relationship one has with the heavenly Father. Does God want you to have this or that? Maybe or maybe not! Why don't you ask the Holy Spirit who is truly the only One that can unveil those secrets to your human spirit? Yielding your rights is putting everything you hold "dear" at the altar of sacrifice. Once offered, then a certain time of waiting is required. Then be on the lookout or listen to the voice of God. You will always find the answer, if you are truly looking for God's answer!

All for Jesus, All for Jesus.
All for Jesus! all for Jesus!
All my being's ransom'd pow'rs;
All my thoughts and words and doings,
All my days and all my hours.
All for Jesus! all for Jesus!
All my days and all my hours.

Let my hands perform his bidding;
Let my feet run in his ways;
Let my eyes see Jesus only;
Let my lips speak forth his praise.
All for Jesus! all for Jesus!
Let my lips speak forth his praise.

Worldlings prize their gems of beauty,
Cling to gilded toys of dust,
Boast of wealth, and fame, and pleasure;
Only Jesus will I trust.
Only Jesus! only Jesus!
Only Jesus will I trust.

Since my eyes were fixed on Jesus,
I've lost sight of all beside,--

So enchained my spirit's vision,
Looking at the crucified.
All for Jesus! all for Jesus!
All for Jesus, crucified!

Oh, what wonder! how amazing!
Jesus, glorious King of kings,
Deigns to call me his beloved,
Lets me rest beneath his wings.
All for Jesus! all for Jesus!
Resting now beneath his wings. - Author Mary D. James

• Allow the press to do its perfect work.

When we think of being tested by the Lord for greater fruitfulness, the next question that follows is usually, "How long will the process take?"

If the Lord starts on Monday, will He be done by Friday afternoon? Or do we even have a clue of the starting time and ending of God's process of testing in our lives?

My answer to this (at least from where I have stood) is that God is not really concerned about the timing, as much as we are. He is not on a time card or even subject to a human calendar. God is after "a thing." This "thing" is called a heart that is surrendered and yielded; a heart that has learned what true disposition is.

No longer question what God is after. All He wants is you – all of you! Your heart, mind, and soul.

Once God has all of you – He will be able to move you to places and situations where you will be highly favored by Him. Remember, He only favors those who favor Him! The rest live on the pure mercy and lovingkindness of the Lord.

Only the Broken Have Fire!

Until God has crushed you and beaten you, then the oil will come forth. The real manifestation of fire will be seen in you and through you when oil has been applied to the lamp (the lamp is you).

A burning fire is not something you find on the "For Sale" table! It is not something that you can acquire by attending a particular gathering. True heavenly fire makes itself known when you have come to the place of total brokenness and the oil has been squeezed out from out of you. Then and only then, can you experience this eternal fire that I have been speaking about.

Chapter 3

The Altar and God's Fire!

"Then the fire of the Lord fell and consumed the burnt sacrifice, and the wood and the stones and the dust, and it licked up the water that was in the trench. Now when all the people saw it, they fell on their faces; and they said, 'The Lord, He is God! The Lord, He is God!'" (1 Kings 18:38, 39)

As we have been looking at the fire of God and how the vessel must be prepared to contain it, it is vital to note that, unless God's divine order is in place, God's fire will not come or be present. There are too many religious forms out there that are done in the name of the Lord, and most of them are to no avail.

When I speak of religious forms, my mind takes me to all the "silly games" many church leaders are putting on today. It almost seems like a three-ringed circus. Much of what is done in the name of the Lord is nothing more than a fleshly spectacular on how to "wow" the crowds and bring them in for a weekly show.

It is true that in society today, people are seeking for a touch of God, a real significance to the nature of God. This is definitely true. Yet, what the institution called "church" has to offer, is mere empty words, motivational clichés, and preachers that are flaunting their fancy footwork. As the late David Wilkerson said one day, *"It makes God vomit!"*

Faltering Between Two Opinions!

"So Ahab sent for all the children of Israel, and gathered the prophets together on Mount Carmel. And Elijah came to all the people, and said, 'How long will you falter between two opinions? If the Lord is God, follow Him; but if Baal, follow him.' But the people answered him not a word. Then Elijah said to the people, 'I alone am left a prophet of the Lord; but Baal's prophets are four hundred and fifty men. Therefore let them give us two bulls; and let them choose one bull for themselves, cut it in pieces, and lay it on the wood, but put no fire under it; and I will prepare the other bull, and lay it on the wood, but put no fire under it. Then you call on the name of your gods, and I will call on the name of the Lord; and the God who answers by fire, He is God.'" (1 Kings 18:20-24)

There came a time in Israel where they had backslidden and given themselves over to the idol worship of Baal. God's people had gone after other gods, and now were seriously involved in idol worship (which, by the way, God hates with great passion).

It was at this time that Elijah, the Prophet of God, came to God's people and said to them, "How long will you falter between two opinions? If the Lord is God, follow Him; but if Baal, follow him." To this comment, the people stayed quiet. Why? I believe that God's people had not been confronted by a man full of fire!

Elijah, Man of Fire!

A man of fire, will always set everything around him on fire! Elijah was a man of fire. Elijah was on a mission to overthrow everything that was out of divine order! Only men or women of fire have this anointing. Only men and women of fire will put themselves in such a fiery furnace!

When you study the life of Elijah, you will find that he was just an ordinary man. As a matter of fact, we know that to be true. In James, it says that **"Elijah was a human being with a nature such as we have; [with feelings, affections, and a constitution like ours] and he prayed earnestly for it not to rain, and no rain fell on the earth for three years and six months. And [then] he prayed again and the heavens supplied rain and the land produced its crops [as usual]."** (James 5:17, 18)

Elijah challenged the four hundred fifty prophets of Baal to a duel. The challenge was that whoever could make fire fall upon the sacrifice – he would be God! What a dare on his part to challenge these false prophets. It was one versus four hundred fifty! Was it really a challenge? Or was it a set up to embarrass the false prophets of Baal. I think the latter.

When a man knows God as a friend, as was the case with Elijah, you know things about God that few others know. The secrets of the Lord are with those who know God. Of course, Elijah knew that fire would fall on his behalf. It takes a God of fire to send fire; it takes a man of fire – to send fire! Elijah was that man!

Divine Order for Fire

"Now Elijah said to the prophets of Baal, 'Choose one bull for yourselves and prepare it first, for you are many; and call on the name of your god, but put no fire under it.'

So they took the bull which was given them, and they prepared it, and called on the name of Baal from morning even

till noon, saying, 'O Baal, hear us!' But there was no voice; no one answered. Then they leaped about the altar which they had made. And so it was, at noon, that Elijah mocked them and said, 'Cry aloud, for he is a god; either he is meditating, or he is busy, or he is on a journey, or perhaps he is sleeping and must be awakened.' So they cried aloud, and cut themselves, as was their custom, with knives and lances, until the blood gushed out on them. And when midday was past, they prophesied until the time of the offering of the evening sacrifice. But there was no voice; no one answered, no one paid attention."** (1 Kings 18:25-29)

There were two bulls set up for this challenge. The prophets of Baal did their arrangements and started to call for fire from Baal. **"So they took the bull which was given them, and they prepared it, and called on the name of Baal from morning even till noon, saying, 'O Baal, hear us!'**

But there was no voice; no one answered. Then they leaped about the altar which they had made. All day long passed and still no fire! All through the day, nothing happened – no answer from Baal, no fire from Baal.

Too many times we see that in ministries. There is a lot of movement and pleading for revival, but no fire. I have seen pastors make the proper arrangements, cool rituals, beautiful buildings, amazing sound systems, and incredible stage presence, but His presence – nowhere to be found. No fire! Why not?

Elijah's Turn

"Then Elijah said to all the people, 'Come near to me.' So

all the people came near to him. And he repaired the altar of the Lord that was broken down. And Elijah took twelve stones, according to the number of the tribes of the sons of Jacob, to whom the word of the Lord had come, saying, "Israel shall be your name." Then with the stones, he built an altar in the name of the Lord; and he made a trench around the altar large enough to hold two seahs of seed. And he put the wood in order, cut the bull in pieces, and laid it on the wood, and said, 'Fill four waterpots with water, and pour it on the burnt sacrifice and on the wood.' Then he said, 'Do it a second time,' and they did it a second time; and he said, 'Do it a third time,' and they did it a third time. So the water ran all around the altar; and he also filled the trench with water. And it came to pass, at the time of the offering of the evening sacrifice, that Elijah the prophet came near and said, 'Lord God of Abraham, Isaac, and Israel, let it be known this day that You are God in Israel and I am Your servant, and that I have done all these things at Your word. Hear me, O Lord, hear me, that this people may know that You are the Lord God, and that You have turned their hearts back to You again.' Then the fire of the Lord fell and consumed the burnt sacrifice, and the wood and the stones and the dust, and it licked up the water that was in the trench. Now when all the people saw it, they fell on their faces; and they said, 'The Lord, He is God! The Lord, He is God!'" (1 Kings 18:30-39)

There Cannot Be Fire Without a Repaired Altar

"Then Elijah said to all the people, 'Come near to me.' So all the people came near to him. And he repaired the altar of the Lord that was broken down."

Listen to this wonderful testimony. Elijah called everyone to come near (as it was his turn to lit the sacrifice,) and watch what God was about to do. One outstanding thing here and worthy to be noted, was that Elijah repaired the altar that was broken down. This is a key step if there is to be any fire anywhere!

The word repaired is used for this passage, and the Hebrew word for repaired is raphe, which the root meaning is or means to heal: — become fresh, completely healed.

Anyone knows that an altar can be repaired, but to be healed? Only a sick person or animal can be healed, not an altar! Or can it?

The writer of 1 Kings said that Elijah repaired or better yet, healed the altar. The word repaired also means to become fresh. There is nothing more important to the human heart than a fresh place for God to demonstrate His power and presence! Once the heart is healed, revival is inevitable.

This is exactly one of the main reasons that revivals don't happen in churches or in the land today. There is no healing taking place at the altar of sacrifice. No one is looking internally for the answer; everyone is looking externally for it. They are building brick upon brick; idea upon idea; and as good as it sounds it is all without fire. We have altars with no fire, because our altars are not healed, they are not fresh! God will not come to an unrepaired, unhealed altar!

Now for the Healing Experience

Healing starts in the inner-man. Nothing is more valuable and more important to the human soul, then a healed heart. True repentance is the beginning of healing. When a person truly repents before God, there will be a cleansing effect coming down from the blood of Jesus upon that man or woman. Once the blood has been applied, that soul is one-hundred percent justified before a holy God!

Along with the effect of cleansing upon that soul, there is also a release of deep disposition to never do anything again from your own power. In other words, the disposition to sin again will be gone! This is how you know when someone has been touched by God's fire.

This new experience of freshness in you, is really what make the fire of God come down upon the human heart over and over again. When the heart is sick, the fire ceases! When the heart is well, it becomes a platform for God's fire.

Nothing Can Quench the Fire of God

"Then the fire of the Lord fell and consumed the burnt sacrifice, and the wood and the stones and the dust, and it licked up the water that was in the trench."

One important thing that I have learned about the spiritual realm is this: Anything that is born from within, where the spirit-man lives, cannot be silenced! You may not obey the prompting, you may disregard the voice that calls you, but His voice is like a fire within. It will not be quenched by your disobedience. You might just have to live with the conviction of disobedience, or obey and live peaceably with God's Spirit.

You can put water on the wood, the sacrifice, on the stones and dust – but when the fire comes, it doesn't respect any of those obstacles. It will consume anything that is not of the Lord and set the sacrifice on fire!

Chapter 4

The Expression of Light!

"I am the Light of the World." (John 8:12)

"You are the Light of the World." (Matthew 5:14a)

As we continue to unveil the secret power of living a life of fire, a life that is never quenched, we must look at two very important and unchanging truths.

The first truth is a bold statement made by Jesus. In the book of John, Jesus said, **"Then Jesus again spoke to them, saying, 'I am the Light of the world; he who follows Me will not walk in the darkness, but will have the Light of life.'"** (John 8:36)

As Jesus opened His mouth to make this bold declaration, I can only imagine the wicked powers of darkness cringing. I am sure all hell begin to tremble at the sound of His voice as it released or unveiled the greatest secret kept for generations. The secret that the Light had come into the world to set the captives free from darkness!

Jesus said that He was the Light of the world!

The picture here is of a lamp that is lit in a room, and it releases the wonder of brightness into a room that has been dominated by darkness.

Literally Dominated by Darkness.

When Jesus begins to make these declarations, He also adds, **"He who follows Me will not walk in the darkness, but will have the Light of life."**

Do you see this? Jesus who is the Light of the world, literally says that he who has this light will not walk in darkness, but will have this same light himself! In other words, the light that is in Jesus because Jesus is Light - is the same Light that will be in anyone who chooses to follow Him.

The Transferring of Light

As we accept Christ into our hearts, His Spirit enters our spirit, and the miracle of the new birth takes place, just like that! We are made alive and our ability to see and make sense of life, is altered; our hearts are cleansed because of the blood of Jesus Christ our Lord. We are now a new creation in Christ. How awesome is that?

The Light has now begun to live in our own heart and life. We are now beaming testimonies of the grace and goodness of God. We didn't deserve it, but God in His mercy, took us in and adopted us as His children. Glory be to the King of kings!

I am not sure how all this mystery takes place, but it is good enough for me. I confessed that I was living a life of selfishness; I wanted to drive my own life and be my own boss. I actually did pretty good; I managed to make it look good on a social level, but sadly, never made it upward to God. One day I heard the truth about Jesus Christ, thus I believed. I received His forgiveness, and I gave Him my life. As a consequence, Christ now lives in me and I in Him! It is that simple.

Responsible to Shine!

One thing I learned about my born-again experience, was that I felt I needed to let everyone around me know, about my new-found faith in Christ. Some heard me and laughed. Some said that they didn't need it. Others, just simply ignored me, and finally, others tried to embarrass me. They said I was crazy, but I knew they were! Whatever your case may be – you are called to shine. You have a responsibility to do it as light in a dark world.

Listen to these words out of the mouth of Jesus: **"You are the light of the world. A city that is set on a hill cannot be hidden. Nor do they light a lamp, and put it under a basket, but on a lampstand, and it gives light to all who are in the house. Let your light so shine before men, that they may see your good works and glorify your Father in heaven."** (Matthew 5:14-16)

The statement becomes a commandment when you first hear the words of Christ. **"You are the light of the world,"** He said.

Once you hear what you are in Christ, then you must proceed to the second part, **"A lamp is not put under a basket, but on a lampstand!"**

We are all called to be on a lampstand (a high point of sorts). This is a place where we can shine that light for major impact: the place of influence, where one can be a testimony of and for the glory of God. This is the reason why we do our best to be the best employee, student, citizen, etc. – so that we may get the promotion and develop some leverage when we lead and have the opportunity to influence for God's glory.

Finally, we reach the third part, the literal command. Jesus said, **"Let your light so shine before men, that they may see your good works and glorify your Father in heaven."**

The call to shine must be done through our lives, expressing Christ to the world.

An intimate life of prayer and devotion has a way of transforming the human mind and spirit. As one gets filled and refilled with God's glory and fire, one will be ready to express it as well. This is so vital - being that one cannot give what he does not have!

While getting more of Jesus in your life, you will inevitably, begin to shine for the Lord. You really don't have to push your way into people's lives. People, by nature, need light. When they see the fire in you, they will want it. They will need some warmth for their cold life; and if not, they will need a lamp to light their path due to ignorance and confusion because of darkness in their lives. Sooner than later, they will come knocking at your door, as you shine for Jesus!

Light: An Expression of His Nature

When I think of Christ and His amazing work which He did by coming into the world as a humble servant and offering His life as a ransom for all humanity, not to mention the fact that He also planted eternity in our hearts, I am in awe of the splendor of my King!

As the Lord moves into our hearts, His presence, His essence, and His fire are released within us. We are now glowing with

His light and our countenance shows it. Listen to the Psalmist say, **"For with You is the fountain of life; In Your light we see light."** (Psalm 36:9)

It is inevitable for the one who truly enters into Christ not to shine with the brightness of His splendor "in the world" he lives in.

When one draws near in contriteness of heart, and with a broken spirit, God's eternal flame will consume them! The results will be astounding. The fire that burns from the throne, will be transferred into that man or woman who position themselves to receive it.

One of my favorite quotes is this one right here: *"It is only by waiting before the throne of grace that we become endued with the Holy Fire. He who waits there long and believingly will imbibe that fire and come forth from his communion with God bearing tokens of where he has been."*

As I close this chapter, I want to challenge you to develop a life that produces fire in you. The longer I live, the more I see the spirit of this world making its attempt to keep God's servants in bondage and attached to a lesser portion of what God has intended.

As hard as spiritual exercises may be, we can't afford to live without them! Practicing the presence of God, no matter what anyone says, it is a hard thing to do and takes tremendous discipline.

If you want to be a man or woman of fire; if you desire to an expression of God's nature here on earth, then begin by developing a life of prayer, a life of fasting, a disciplined plan to read and meditate on God's Word, and finally, take time to write in your personal journal what wonderful secrets God shares with you.

Chapter 5

Attending to the Expression! - Part 1

"Negligence is the rust of the soul, that corrodes through all her best resolves."

- Owen Felltham

"And the fire on the altar shall be kept burning on it. It shall not go out, but the priest shall burn wood on it every morning; and he shall lay out the burnt offering on it and offer up in smoke the fat portions of the peace offerings on it." (Leviticus 6:12)

The Scripture I use here gives us an interesting perspective on a few things regarding the theme of this chapter, Attending to the Expression.

For one, it shows us what God truly desires and what God doesn't desire. Secondly, it gives us insight into who it is that should take care of the matter at hand, and how to do it as it seems pleasing unto the Lord.

The concern in the text is fire on the altar. God tells Moses, **"[it] shall be kept burning on it."**

Obviously, the fire is not going to burn by itself. It needs the assistance or the cooperation of a human vessel. God chooses us to partake of His glorious plan!

The priest were then commissioned to **"burn wood on it every**

morning." This was to be done daily if fire was to burn on the altar. What was at stake here? The burnt offering.

One of the things I have learned in my personal walk with God is to pay attention to the Law of Negligence or the Principle of Neglect. I have learned that if one does not attend to a matter – the matter will not resolve itself. This principle applies to everything in life.

In our Christian life, our walk must be of such great importance to us, that we attend to the pillars that make it work, that make it outstanding and vibrant. To not attend to the spiritual disciplines in our Christian walk, is to neglect the benefits that this great life can bring.

Is it any wonder why so many believers are left wondering, struggling or surprised by negative results or when things go wrong around them or in them? Way too often, the reason something collapsed was not because God intended to do it, but the Principle of Neglect took effect and we are only reaping the fruit of it!

Furthermore, God told Moses to make sure that oil be gathered and put in the lamp for its lighting. I am sure you know why. Without oil, there can be no fire. If there is no fire, then the lamp is of no effect and those in the house will be in darkness soon!

As we develop this philosophy of expressing the nature of God into the world, we must attend to the things that makes this real and practical.

I have outlined a few things that I consider to be tools, disciplines, or spiritual exercises that guarantee a life that flows with an eternal fire.

Cultivating a Life of Personal Prayer

I would like to open up before you a subject of which I consider to be one of the most powerful weapons in the Christian life – the subject of personal prayer.

As much as I appreciate the corporate prayer meeting, the fellowship of the brother, and the prayer of the saints – and they all have their place in the body of Christ - it is my firm belief, that nothing compares to the secret life of personal prayer.

Personal prayer is very powerful for all who discipline themselves to practice it.

It is in this secret place of personal prayer that the man or woman of God finds true enrichment in God. Nothing compares to these types of daily very personal encounters with the Holy Spirit.

In times of personal prayer, the believer has to face a few things before entering in. Here is how Jesus outlined it for us in Matthew 6:6 - **"But when you pray, go into your [most] private room, and, closing the door, pray to your Father, Who is in secret; and your Father, Who sees in secret, will reward you in the open."**

Let us look at a few things:

1. But when you pray. When should we pray? I have my preferences. I personally like to meet God early in the morning (usually at 5am) and take my time being in His lovely presence. I do have a time frame that I spend at His feet and it usually runs about two hours daily. I allow myself to enter in and spend much time especially in worship and intercession. I can't tell you what a joy it is to accomplish this daily.

My spiritual father used to tell me, "David, if you arise early in the morning to meet God, 90% of your spiritual war has been won– now walk out the last 10% in full obedience."

2. *Go into your [most] private room.* After you have made up your mind to meet God, then take note of the specific instruction. This will make the difference whether you touch God or not. Your "private" or "secret" room is a spiritual place where you meet God. It has to do with attitude and willingness of heart. Going into your most "private room" means that you are coming into your deepest parts of yourself and allowing God to see ALL of you as you really are!

I really think that the reason most people's prayer lives are ineffective, is due to this one part – not entering into their private room. They show up to prayer, but they never enter in! Do you get me? They are always talking about prayer, prayer meetings, but they never manage to enter in to get the benefit of meeting God face to face! Nothing is more transformational than seeing God face to face.

3. *Closing the door.* Closing the door means that you make a conscious effort to be alone with God. You have purposed in your heart and in your mind that no one will be there with you but God. It is He alone that will be there before you. If the door remains open, your mind and heart, will be distracted by external fears, doubts and worries. Closing the door is actually a sign to God that says, "I'm all yours God; search me in and out!"

4. Pray to your Father who is in the secret. As you close the door of your external world and open the portal to the Father's throne room, He is right there waiting for you with expectation. Faith is required to see this. Without faith you cannot experience the Father!

5. Your Father will reward you in the open. Have you read this? I can hardly fathom the thought of this! As you spend time in the Father's presence, you will be changed! You see, to be in the Father's presence means that you are receiving downloads of who He is. All the while that you are in His presence, there is a transference of His nature into yours. There is an actual metamorphosis taking place as you wait before Him. The reward is His presence. Where ever you go and whatever you do, His fire is inevitable!

One of the most powerful exercises to spiritual power is definitely a life of personal prayer. The next time that you hear of people talking about prayer – take note: Were those people touched by God's fire? Fire is the testimony of being in the secret place with the Father!

Is it easy? No. Is it convenient? No. Is there a right way to pray? Maybe, but I haven't learned it yet. Do I still use an alarm to arise out of sleep...you bet! Do I need it? Everyday! I use anything and everything I can to get me to that secret place to meet my heavenly Father and you should too.

Chapter 6

Attending to the Expression! - Part 2

"Then I said, I will not make mention of him, nor speak any more in his name. But His word was in my heart as a burning fire shut up in my bones, and I was weary from holding it back, and I could not." (Jeremiah 20:9)

The Prophet of God, Jeremiah, without doubt, was touched by God's Word. It was inside of him like a fire shut up in his bones. Can you picture this? Though he tried to hold it back, he couldn't! Friends, this is true fire!

Allowing God's Word into your spiritual life, will definitely make you burn for Jesus. As a matter of fact, to the degree that we allow God's words to permeate and penetrate our spirit, is to the degree that we express His life to others. People can see it, feel it, and experience it through us!

There are so many creative ways of reading God's Word. Some read the Word of God with the intent to study it profoundly; others read the Word of God to pull out life principles directly from the mouth of God; and others, study the characters of the Bible and the great things they accomplished in their lifetime.

I have met people who have memorized extensive parts of Scripture, and they can quote it at any given second quite accurately. This to me, is amazing! My teacher in Bible Geography, would always talk about how interesting it was to study the places, and lands, and cultures of the Bible. In short, I have made some very interesting studies in the different forms and methods of gaining more information. Yet, I have discovered the one area that I am most in love with – meditation!

David said, **"BLESSED (HAPPY, fortunate, prosperous, and enviable) is the man who walks and lives not in the counsel of the ungodly [following their advice, their plans, and purposes] nor stands [submissive and inactive] in the path where sinners walk, nor sits down [to relax and rest] where the scornful [and the mockers] gather. But his delight and desire are in the law of the Lord, and on His law (the precepts, the instructions, the teachings of God) he habitually meditates (ponders and studies) by day and by night. And he shall be like a tree firmly planted [and tended] by the streams of water, ready to bring forth its fruit in its season; its leaf also shall not fade or wither; and everything he does shall prosper [and come to maturity]."** (Psalm 1:1-3 Amplified Version Bible)

Cultivating a Life of Reading & Meditating on God's Word

David, the Psalmist, made a powerful statement about the individual who doesn't waste his life with the foolishness of an ungodly lifestyle. He said that he spends his time "meditating" on God's Word. What exactly does it mean to meditate? Let's look at it.

Webster's Dictionary has it written this way - meditate: to engage in contemplation or reflection. To engage in mental exercise for the purpose of reaching a heightened level of spiritual awareness. Also, it means to focus one's thoughts: to reflect on or ponder. Finally, it can mean to plan or project in the mind.

A time of meditation on God's Word would simply be to take a portion of Scripture and contemplate seriously on it, reflect on it by reviewing it over and over and over again, until your whole being is captivated by it.

When spending time in my own meditation of God's Word, I like to read on a daily basis a small portion of Scripture. I will read it with my mind focused on the possibility that God wants to say something to me. So with my spirit open to His, and my mind focused on His every word that I'm "pondering," plus my heart in tune with His emotions, I venture into my journey.

After spending quite some time doing this repeatedly in my secret place of prayer, the Lord will disclose or unveil His heart to me. It is here where I learn a new principle to apply, a correction in my own life, a command that I must persist in developing, a thought that will align my attitude with His, or simply rediscovering His fresh love which He has over me! There is nothing in the world that compares to this experience, nothing!

While the world runs here and there pursuing vain things that produce no lasting impact, I'd rather sit at the Master's table and learn about me, about Him, and about all the wonderful things He has prepared for those who fear Him! Priceless.

Bible Reading Plans

I think every believer should get a hold of a good bible reading plan. What do you have to lose? With a plan, you can reach your goal of reading the whole Bible in a year or more; without a plan you will most likely fall short in completing your reading of this sacred text.

Many chose to read one book at a time, which is not a bad idea, if you can stick to it. Others like to start from the very beginning and work themselves through the whole Bible till they complete it, which is also a very good idea, if completed.

Now, because of human nature, people tend to not be very disciplined. They often start fast, but don't finish what they start. I'm sure you have been there. I have! To combat this, I personally have adopted into my reading plan, a "Read the Bible in a Year Plan." I have used it for more than 30 years, and it has served me well. The plan that I presently use offers this: A chapter on the Old Testament, a Psalm, a chapter of the gospels, and a chapter of the Pauline Epistles. Going through it on a daily basis, guarantees me a read of the whole Bible in a year.

To be more specific, I have tailored this plan to reading the Bible once every three years. This allows me to do my meditations with greater effectiveness because I am not rushed to finish the listing of daily chapters. So, I only read a little bit daily. I meditate on God's heart daily. It is not really about how much you read, but how much you allow the Spirit of God and the Word to take over your life.

Cultivating a Life of Personal Journaling

Personal Journaling is truly an amazing way to cultivate and develop yourself as you meditate upon God's Word. Taking notes of thoughts that can transform you and others is really something that brings God's prophetic Word to life and establishes you in so many ways.

Why would anyone want to write the thoughts that he or she

encounters?

Well for one, when you write the things that you discover, they tend to be remembered better when they are hand-written. If you value a thought, you will write it down. If you don't value a thought, then you will leave it alone and never revisit it again. Wisdom is truly reserved for those who seek for it!

Another thing that Personal Journaling does for you is hold you accountable. Everything you write is staring you in the face. Will you follow it? Will you put it into practice in your own life? Do you really believe it? Etc.

One thing I have noticed is that people who take good notes usually are people with calm spirits, they are orderly in thought and typically live very tranquil lives. Just saying.

Through personal prayer and meditation, one can truly avail themselves of this fire that God gives. The fire will be started by your broken spirit before God, but to maintain it, to keep the expression going – it will take some work! I have discovered that by working through these two practices, one can stay burning daily. I venture to say that if one does it consistently, there is no knowing of the potential of what this vessel can be for God in years to come!

PART 2

WHAT HAPPENED TO THE FIRE?

Lessons on How the Fire was Lost.

Chapter 7

Where did the Fire Go?

**"To the angel of the church of Ephesus write,
'These things says He who holds the seven stars in His right
hand, who walks in the midst of the seven golden lamp-
stands: I know your works, your labor, your patience, and
that you cannot bear those who are evil. And you have tested
those who say they are apostles and are not, and have found
them liars; and you have persevered and have patience, and
have labored for My name's sake and have not become weary. Nevertheless I have this against you, that you have left
your first love. Remember therefore from where you have
fallen; repent and do the first works, or else I will come to
you quickly and remove your lampstand from its place—unless you repent.'"** (Revelation 2:1-5)

In times past when I have meditated upon this passage, I always
turn my attention to the point where it says, **"…you have left
your first love."** I don't know about you, but I have seen how
this part seems to take the whole focus of the verse.

Leaving your first love is only the fruit of something much deeper. It doesn't answer the question of why the "first love" was left
behind or lost. It doesn't reveal how careless one can become
with their practice of Christianity, nor how one neglects what is
truly valuable.

Meditating upon the notes for this manuscript, I started to go
deeper in study and questioned how is it that one can actually get

to the place where he or she loses the original motivating factor for all they can do for God?!

Being that my subject matter has to do with God's fire burning bright in us and through us, I want to point out in this chapter how one can lose such a holy fire, and consequently abort the reason for what and why it has been given.

Attending to the Externals

Obviously, our walk and service to God has to do with manifesting who we are, and how we let our light shine in this dark world. We have been called to this. Everyone who has been called to walk with God has this mission – to be a light!

I don't believe that this is the matter in question here, but I do believe that it is more a matter of priority than the doing of good works.

If we turn our attention to the verse mentioned above, we will quickly discover that the Lord who walks in the midst of His church is pretty pleased with the external work the church of Ephesus had been doing. He pointed out that their labor and patience coupled with their hatred for evil was impeccable.

From this perspective, the church of Ephesus would get a "gold star," if you will. They would be considered the church that went "above and beyond" their call of duty. Yes, the Master was pleased with the work of their hands – but not with the work of their hearts!

Isn't this the issue with most of our modern portrayal of Christianity? Isn't this what most churches are "playing for?" To be recognized for their stand against evil, against false doctrines, etc. Some go further and make their sanctuaries concert halls (in the name of relevancy) with the goal to occupy and fill every chair in their sanctuary. Somehow, external works have a way of placing a church in some type of status or on a pedestal.

Though many pastors and leaders say that they are not going after the masses, they are! Some for godly kingdom-agenda reasons, but the majority for ego-driven reasons! To this Jesus comes and says, **"I know your works, your labor, your patience, and that you cannot bear those who are evil. And you have tested those who say they are apostles and are not and have found them liars; and you have persevered, and have patience, and have labored for My name's sake, and have not become weary. Nevertheless, I have this against you, that you have left your first love."**

In layman's terms this means, "You have done well doing good works outside, but have failed miserably doing good works inside your own heart!"

The love is gone; the fire is gone! There is nothing left of what was there when you first started doing the work.

Matter of Priority!

If one desires to please the Lord, they must first learn that pleasing the Lord has to start in the developing of a deep love for God. Pleasing God starts with loving Him with all our hearts!

The next thing would be to keep a consistency of this love flowing. It sounds easy, but it is not! There are many other distractions that will come between you and your love for God. It will be a challenge, if you don't understand this type of battle you are in.

Lastly, to keep this love fresh and vibrant, meeting with God in the secret place of prayer as a daily standard, will give you this ability. It will stabilize you and keep you going for the rest of your days.

You must spend time in the fire to have the fire!

What Mary Knew!

"Now it happened as they went, that He entered a certain village; and a certain woman named Martha welcomed Him into her house. And she had a sister called Mary, who also sat at Jesus' feet and heard His word. But Martha was distracted with much serving, and she approached Him and said, 'Lord, do You not care that my sister has left me to serve alone? Therefore tell her to help me.'

And Jesus answered and said to her, 'Martha, Martha, you are worried and troubled about many things. But one thing is needed, and Mary has chosen that good part, which will not be taken away from her.'" (Luke 10:38-42)

If there is something we can appreciate about this story – is that we have the privilege of seeing both sides to it. We see the life of Mary, and we also see the life of Martha displayed in real time. Two sisters, yet very different in spiritual posture.

Mary appears to be a student of Jesus. A woman who is humble and teachable in spirit. She was attentive to the divine words of Jesus. How do you think that a person who longs to be like Christ, will not be acknowledged by God? Obviously, she longed to have what Jesus had!

Now Mary's sister, Martha, was a bit different in the sense that she seemed a bit more occupied with the other aspect of ministry – the serving part. It is not a bad thing! Many have made Martha out to be the "bad guy," but she is really not. We as believers need to serve! We need to spend time in serving and helping out our those around us. Absolutely!

So what is the deal?

The deal is that we have two different types of personalities presented here, and we also have two types of philosophies portrayed. One is to sit and learn; the other is give and serve. Are these actions right? Is one more valuable than the other? The answer is yes! They are both right and they are both valuable. They only differ in priority.

As valuable as both of these two things are, we must make the conscious choice to prioritize them. Jesus said that to love the Lord was to be first; loving your neighbor would be second.

Being in the presence of Jesus till He directs us in some way, must always be first. If we don't get our ideas from God, then it will lack the fire. It is when God speaks to our hearts that the fire is turned on. If we do "good works" for the sake of the works themselves, then we really don't have fire to keep it going. It will eventually all settle and die!

Mary understood the value of sitting at the feet of Jesus. She knew that everything came from a fountain and understood that Christ was the Fountain!

On the other hand, Martha, was a true servant. She wanted to make sure that everything was "just right!" The Scripture says that she was, "distracted with much serving," and Jesus even said, "…You are worried and troubled about many things."

If you are serving God and the work has begun to wear you down to the point where you become distracted, worried, and troubled, then my friend, you are neglecting your first love.

Though both things are valuable, to only one of the sisters Jesus gave praise to, her name was Mary. Jesus said of her: **"But one thing is needed, and Mary has chosen that good part, which will not be taken away from her."**

Chapter 8

Samson: The Man Who Unveiled His Heart to the Devil!

"For behold, you shall conceive and bear a son. And no razor shall come upon his head, for the child shall be a Nazirite to God from the womb; and he shall begin to deliver Israel out of the hand of the Philistines." (Judges 13:1)

"So the woman bore a son and called his name Samson; and the child grew, and the Lord blessed him. And the Spirit of the Lord began to move upon him at Mahaneh Dan between Zorah and Eshtaol." (Judges 13:24-25)

Meditating upon the subject of this book called Inextinguishable, I have come to realize that when God does reach out and touch our lives – this touch is with such holy jealousy. God means business and will keep every word of promise to us!

I have often wondered the "why" and the "how" a person can turn away from such a touch, being that it is of supernatural kind; yet many are challenged to keep themselves in the flow of God's fire.

As I have written in previous places in this writing, one is truly responsible for the gift of life God has given. One is to be a steward of the fire of God in their lives. I have no doubt that man must keep His way by guarding everything precious God has placed in his or her care.

Born Out of Barrenness

In this chapter, I want to bring out the life of Samson. Samson was a very distinguished figure in the kingdom of God. Though he was one hundred percent man, Samson was not your ordinary servant of the Lord. He had been chosen by the Lord to carry out some specific instructions.

In chapter 13 of the Book of Judges, we discover a few things that will be of great interest. For one, God's people had lost their way again and were no longer walking in the favor of the Lord. To sin and fall into the enemy's hands because of God's judgment had become an occurrence way to common for them. After being in the enemy's bondage for a season, they would cry out and God would raise up a deliverer to get them out of bondage. They would then continue for another season of walking in repentance, then fall again. This went on for years.

It was during one of these bondages to the Philistines (which lasted 40 years) that God sent an angel to speak to Manoah's wife, (who would later become Samson's mother.) Up until this time, Manoah's wife had been unable to bare children.

It was then, that the Angel of the Lord appeared to her and said, **"Indeed now, you are barren and have borne no children, but you shall conceive and bear a son. Now therefore, please be careful not to drink wine or similar drink, and not to eat anything unclean. For behold, you shall conceive and bear a son. And no razor shall come upon his head, for the child shall be a Nazirite to God from the womb; and he shall begin to deliver Israel out of the hand of the Philistines."** (Judges 13:3-5)

Can you imagine this scenario? What a revelation from God. Manoah's wife was in great disbelief to all this. She quickly tells her husband about this powerful manifestation, which caused him to urge God for "a repeat" of this event.

It was here that God answered his prayer and revealed Himself one more time. He gave them both instruction on how to raise their newborn son who would be called Samson; he would be under a Nazarite vow.

"So the woman bore a son and called his name Samson; and the child grew, and the Lord blessed him. And the Spirit of the Lord began to move upon him at Mahaneh Dan between Zorah and Eshtaol." (Judges 13:24-25)

The Scripture tells us that Samson was born out of a barren womb. It says that he grew, and the Lord blessed him. It also says that the Spirit of the Lord began to move upon him.

Obviously, God has a plan for this man, as the Lord had established him and had set His heart on fire to do His work.

Strange Doors of Opportunity!

It came to pass in chapter 14 that Samson went to Timnah. Why would Samson go and hang out in Philistine country? If he well knew that the Philistines were the enemies of Israel, why did he go out there? Well, let's find out….

As Samson visits this place, he finds a woman of one of the daughters of the Philistines that he likes very much. He tells his parents that he likes her and wants her. Obviously, the parents disagree and give Samson other options for finding a wife among his own people.

Though the parents didn't understand why Samson felt this way about this woman from Timnah, they eventually allowed it. The Scripture then says, that it was God who was behind all of this. How about this for those who hold strict theology on what holiness is? Listen to this word: **"But his father and mother did not know that it was of the Lord—that He was seeking an occasion to move against the Philistines. For at that time the Philistines had dominion over Israel."** (Judges 14:4)

The Riddle!

After this event, God kept on working. While in Timnah, Samson had some great exploits. Samson eventually got married and posed his infamous riddle. It was through this one riddle that he challenged the thirty men at his wedding and made a bet with them. **"Then Samson said to them, 'Let me pose a riddle to you. If you can correctly solve and explain it to me within the seven days of the feast, then I will give you thirty linen garments and thirty changes of clothing. But if you cannot explain it to me, then you shall give me thirty linen garments and thirty changes of clothing.'"** (Judges 14:12-13)

What was so significant about this riddle? It seemed like nothing - yet God used it to further magnify the possibilities of greater conflict with the Philistines.

It was then that the thirty men could not figure the riddle that they consequently threatened Samson's wife. They enticed her and asked her to figure out the riddle by asking her husband.

They ordered her to do this or her and her father's house would be burnt.

She pleaded and pleaded with Samson until he told her the riddle. It was here that Samson got very angry; just listen to the Word: **"Then the Spirit of the Lord came upon him mightily, and he went down to Ashkelon and killed thirty of their men, took their apparel, and gave the changes of clothing to those who had explained the riddle. So his anger was aroused, and he went back up to his father's house. And Samson's wife was given to his companion, who had been his best man."** (Judges 14:19-20)

Here is a man of fire– a man of deep calling and conviction. Samson is a man under command and is being challenged to a life of higher integrity and composure. He lost the bet he had made using the riddle, and he lost his wife to his companion. He was furious!

When we allow hurt and pain to have its way in us, we open ourselves to so many other dangers. Once we get out of control in our spirit – anything can happen if we are not measuring our walk with wisdom.

Samson is Challenged Again!

"After a while, in the time of wheat harvest, it happened that Samson visited his wife with a young goat. And he said, 'Let me go in to my wife, into her room.' But her father would not permit him to go in. Her father said, 'I really thought that you thoroughly hated her; therefore I gave her to your companion. Is not her younger sister better than she? Please,

take her instead.'" (Judges 15:1, 2)

After his anger subsided from losing his bet with the thirty men, he came back to look for his wife. To his surprise, his wife had been given over to his best man. This didn't sit well with Samson, and he was angry one more time.

Do you see what is happening here? When a man will not control his own spirit, he will end up falling into countless mishaps. We must guard ourselves from all of this and take heed to our spirit.

When Samson heard his ex-father-in-law tell him that his wife had been given over to the best man, he became very upset and swore to destroy the Philistines. He tied three-hundred foxes tail to tail and set them on fire. The foxes ran into the grain fields and burnt everything in their path. The Philistines then questioned who had done this and took revenge on Samson's ex-wife and father-in-law.

"Samson said to them, 'Since you would do a thing like this, I will surely take revenge on you, and after that I will cease.' So he attacked them hip and thigh with a great slaughter; then he went down and dwelt in the cleft of the rock of Etam.'" (Judges 15:7-8)

Samson again swore to take revenge on the Philistines and would not stop until he would accomplish his purpose.

He was arrested by his own people and taken into custody. It was agreed that his own people would turn him in into the hands of the Philistines. He was bound in ropes, and when the Philistines saw him, they shouted and rushed towards him. The Spirit of the Lord came upon Samson, and he took the jaw of a donkey and killed one-thousand of them. Then he ruled as judge for the next twenty years.

Eleven Pieces of Silver!

Now, Samson was not a "saint." He struggled with women. This is obvious to see by reading the Scripture, **"Now Samson went to Gaza and saw a harlot there and went in to her."** (Judges 16:1)

He was into harlots and all kinds of illicit things. His parents did not support this, and when it came to marrying that woman from Timnah– we see him once again messing around with another harlot.

What does that say to you? It tells us that there is a controversy in the center of this man's life. Yes, Samson is anointed; yes, Samson is powerful in God; but Samson is also a "sitting duck" for the enemy and a target to the seduction and strategy of the enemy.

"Afterward it happened that he loved a woman in the Valley of Sorek, whose name was Delilah. And the lords of the Philistines came up to her and said to her, 'Entice him, and find out where his great strength lies, and by what means we may overpower him, that we may bind him to afflict him; and every one of us will give you eleven hundred pieces of silver.'" (Judges 16:4-5)

The enemy was on a rampage and was not going to stop charging against God's servant – at least not until he found out how to bring him down and destroy him. This is always the enemy's goal – to shut down God's instrument!

The enemy couldn't find the perfect opportunity in the life of Samson up to this point. The enemy had already tried anger, rage, jealousy, and lust to try and stop God's vessel, but all to no avail. Then it happened!

Samson had an issue with a lot of things but had managed to keep himself away from idolatry or at least from compromising his own heart and give himself to anything other than Jehovah God. After all, Samson was a man of Nazarite vow and mightily anointed!

The Scripture tells us in chapter 16 of Judges that Samson loved a woman in the Valley of Sorek, whose name was Delilah. This was the woman chosen by Satan himself or hand-picked by the devil, to do all she could to bring Samson down!

Here is what the devil is after in every man or woman of God:

1. Where great strength lies in us;
2. Different means to overpower us;
3. With the purpose to bind and afflict us.

Delilah was paid some serious money to uncover the secret behind Samson's life. Was the man powerful? Yes, he was! Was he mighty in God? Yes, he was! Was he a keeper of the Nazarite vow? Yes, he was! So obviously, Samson was going to be challenged to the core of his spiritual being!

Unveiling Your Heart to the Devil

"Then she said to him, 'How can you say, I love you, when your heart is not with me? You have mocked me these three times and have not told me where your great strength lies.' And it came to pass, when she pestered him daily with her words and pressed him, so that his soul was vexed to death, that he told her all his heart, and said to her, 'No razor has ever come upon my head, for I have been a Nazirite to God from my mother's womb. If I am shaven, then my strength will leave me, and I shall become weak, and be like any other man.' When Delilah saw that he had told her all his heart, she sent and called for the lords of the Philistines, saying, 'Come up once more, for he has told me all his heart.'" (Judges 16:15-18)

After Delilah's three failed attempts to uncover Samson's power were completed, she finally told him, **"How can you say, I love you, when your heart is not with me? You have mocked me these three times and have not told me where your great strength lies."** (Judges 16:15)

If the enemy tempts our minds, we can easily rebuke the vain imaginations and take authority over any principality and power. Now, when the enemy gets a hold of our heart, and we fall in love with their heart (the idea or the lie) then our lives will be in danger of succumbing to the enemy's tactic and strategy.

The devil would love for us to give up our hearts to him!

He would so love for us to surrender our heart and will to him; in this way, he would more easily dominate our actions and control our destiny!

The enemy will do what Delilah showed us: **"And it came to pass, when she pestered him daily with her words and pressed him, so that his soul was vexed to death, that he told her all his heart..."** (Judges 16:16, 17a)

Here are a couple of characteristics the devil uses in his destructive approach:

1. She *pestered* him with her words
2. She *pressed* him

The word *pestered* means to bring distress. Some people when they speak to us do nothing more than just bring distress upon us. What is distress? Extreme anxiety, sorrow, or pain! Have you had some people bring this upon you?

The word *pressed* means to urge. Anytime in your life that you feel pressed to act, it usually is not God speaking to you. It might be your flesh or the devil, but normally God doesn't urge you to do anything unless He is very specific!

Samson Finally Gives Away the Secret!

"No razor has ever come upon my head, for I have been a Nazirite to God from my mother's womb. If I am shaven, then my strength will leave me, and I shall become weak, and be like any other man." (Judges 16:17)

After much applied pressure from Delilah, Samson gave away the great secret to his great power. My friends, this was the beginning of the end for this servant of God. What was at stake here? God's favor! God's anointing! God's protection! God's Vision!

Once the Nazarite vow was broken, the power left Samson.

I believe God entrusts to all of us His children—His anointing. He prepares a certain calling for each of us, but for this to be carried out to its full potential, one must also become and remain that special vessel God called it to be! Samson ceased to be this vessel.

The Power is Gone!

"And she said, 'The Philistines are upon you, Samson!' So he awoke from his sleep, and said, 'I will go out as before, at other times, and shake myself free!' But he did not know that the Lord had departed from him." (Judges 16:20)

Once Delilah put Samson to sleep, she had a Philistine come and shave his head. While Samson slept, his power left him!

When she told Samson that the Philistines were upon him, he woke up from his sleep, and fully convinced that he was still full of power said to himself, "'I will go out as before, at other times, and shake myself free!' But he did not know that the Lord had departed from him."

Samson never thought about the loss of power. He didn't take the Nazarite vow seriously! He was now enchanted by Delilah and didn't have a clue the Lord was departing him. Isn't this tragic? Isn't this a story for the ages?

No Eyes No Vision!

"Then the Philistines took him and put out his eyes and brought him down to Gaza. They bound him with bronze fetters, and he became a grinder in the prison." (Judges 16:21)

After Samson lost his anointing and power, he also lost his vision. His eyes were put out. He was then bound with bronze fetters and became a grinder in the prison.

Samson lost his anointing, his place in God, his vision and strength were also taken away, plus his ministry was cancelled out, as he grinded in prison.

Was this supposed to have taken place in the life of Samson? Was this God's best for this man under a Nazarite vow? Did God really intend to use Samson as an illustration of a man who lost the fire for God?

The story seems too tragic to read. It is a painful testimony of what happens to an un-surrendered heart— a heart that refuses to yield to God's divine order.

Samson had issues like so many of us, yet his daily sins were only leading him to the big sin of breaking his only source of power, the Nazarite vow!

The enemy begins small and then he gets better acquainted with us that he begins to make bigger demands upon us. He started with anger and rage in the life of Samson; after this he moved to lust. Once he was at this place, he moved on to owning Samson's heart. When the enemy finally got Samson to share his heart with Delilah, the end was not far!

Samson lost his fire because He became lax and negligent in keeping his Nazarite vow to Jehovah God. This is all the enemy ever wanted from Samson, to shut him down! Let this lesson serve us well!

Chapter 9

King Solomon: The Man Who Would Not 'Come Away!'

"So Zadok the priest, Nathan the prophet, Benaiah the son of Jehoiada, the Cherethites, and the Pelethites went down and had Solomon ride on King David's mule, and took him to Gihon. Then Zadok the priest took a horn of oil from the tabernacle and anointed Solomon. And they blew the horn, and all the people said, 'Long live King Solomon!' And all the people went up after him; and the people played the flutes and rejoiced with great joy, so that the earth seemed to split with their sound." (1 Kings 1:38-40)

This is a great start in a man's life. This is what any individual longs for as they begin a new venture or endeavor. Solomon had been chosen as king of Israel to replace his father, David. Everything was in place and Solomon was about to experience the ride of his life!

I remember the day when I was ordained before the District Council of the Assemblies of God in Houston, Texas. It was indeed an unforgettable night. Along with another eight ministers who would be receiving ordination that night, I had never felt so humbled and at the same time privileged to serve God with all my talents, gifts, and all the grace God had afforded me.

As the message was given and the challenge to "preach the word in season and out of season," came forth, my heart felt so empowered. It was the real deal! The rest of the night went just as planned – the laying on of hands by the presbytery, the prophetic words, the anointing with oil, and the receiving of a mantle – it made it so overwhelming. I will forever be grateful to God for allowing me to have experienced that beautiful experience many years ago.

In no way am I comparing myself with Solomon's anointing of King, but I understand some of the emotion that went on as Zadok the priest anointed him with oil.

"God Said, 'Ask! What Shall I Give You?'"

"And Solomon loved the Lord, walking in the statutes of his father David, except that he sacrificed and burned incense at the high places. Now the king went to Gibeon to sacrifice there, for that was the great high place: Solomon offered a thousand burnt offerings on that altar. At Gibeon the Lord appeared to Solomon in a dream by night; and God said, 'Ask! What shall I give you?' And Solomon said, 'You have shown great mercy to Your servant David my father, because he walked before You in truth, in righteousness, and in uprightness of heart with You; You have continued this great kindness for him, and You have given him a son to sit on his throne, as it is this day. Now, O Lord my God, You have made Your servant king instead of my father David, but I am a little child; I do not know how to go out or come in. And Your servant is in the midst of Your people whom You have chosen, a great people, too numerous to be numbered or counted. Therefore give to Your servant an understanding heart to judge Your people, that I may discern between good and evil. For who is able to judge this great people of Yours? The speech pleased the Lord, that Solomon had asked this

thing.' Then God said to him, 'Because you have asked this thing, and have not asked long life for yourself, nor have asked riches for yourself, nor have asked the life of your enemies, but have asked for yourself understanding to discern justice, behold, I have done according to your words; see, I have given you a wise and understanding heart, so that there has not been anyone like you before you, nor shall any like you arise after you. And I have also given you what you have not asked: both riches and honor, so that there shall not be anyone like you among the kings all your days. So if you walk in My ways, to keep My statutes and My commandments, as your father David walked, then I will lengthen your days.' Then Solomon awoke, and indeed it had been a dream. And he came to Jerusalem and stood before the ark of the covenant of the Lord, offered up burnt offerings, offered peace offerings, and made a feast for all his servants." (1 Kings 3:3-15)

These set of Scriptures, begin by saying that **"Solomon loved the Lord."** Oh, the great things God can do in us and through us when our priorities are right! When we find ourselves in alignment with God and His will, all things will go well.

When God finds a person who is willing to be used and that person surrenders totally to God— there is no telling of all that that Lord can accomplish through such a one.

Solomon immediately recognized his own lack before God: He said, **"I am a little child, and I don't know how to go out and come in."**

He understood that God's people were numerous and that his

ability to lead in the flesh was near impossible. So Solomon cried out to God and said, **"Therefore give to Your servant an understanding heart to judge Your people, that I may discern between good and evil."** The Scripture says that the "... speech pleased the Lord."

God Pours Wisdom on Solomon

"Because you have asked this thing, and have not asked long life for yourself, nor have asked riches for yourself, nor have asked the life of your enemies, but have asked for yourself understanding to discern justice, behold, I have done according to your words; see, I have given you a wise and understanding heart, so that there has not been anyone like you before you, nor shall any like you arise after you. And I have also given you what you have not asked: both riches and honor, so that there shall not be anyone like you among the kings all your days." (1 Kings 3:11-14)

God was so truly moved by Solomon's request, that He gave Solomon wisdom and an understanding heart. God told Solomon that there would be no other king before him or after him that would compare to him. Along with wisdom, God promised Solomon riches and honor! Remember what God told Solomon: **"Because you have asked this thing, and have not asked for long life for yourself, nor have asked for riches for yourself, nor have asked the life of your enemies, but have asked for understanding to discern justice..."** (1 Kings 3:11)

The Promise!

In blessing Solomon, God also revealed to him this one note:

"So if you walk in My ways, to keep My statutes and My commandments, as your father David walked, then I will lengthen your days."

The Lord told Solomon that if he walked in all of His ways, that his days would be lengthened. All Solomon had to do was to continue being led by God's words and everything would be established.

After this, Solomon understood God's promise: **"Then Solomon awoke, and indeed it had been a dream. And he came to Jerusalem and stood before the ark of the covenant of the Lord, offered up burnt offerings, offered peace offerings, and made a feast for all his servants."**

Here is something to remember, the law of sowing and reaping is always active as we live out our lives. If we sow good, we will reap good. Whatever we sow, we get. If Solomon walked in God's ways, the kingdom would be established, and his days would be lengthened.

Great Accomplishments

It was evident after this encounter that God's wisdom accompanied King Solomon. He judged well and was highly honored by the Lord.

He had the attention of the world. His wisdom was like nothing ever seen or heard. It was during this time that King Solomon started building the Temple for the Lord. This building project was truly awesome in every way you can think of. It was made of gold and exhibited all kinds of artistry. It was truly phenomenal. This project took him about seven years to complete.

What I want to know is the following: Was King Solomon facing all kinds of temptations while building the House of the Lord? Was he overcome by lust and power? Was he doing his best to suppress it? Makes you wonder... And then the Scripture says that after he was done building the Temple, that he set his heart to build his own house: **"But Solomon took thirteen years to build his own house, so he finished all his house."** (1 Kings 7:1)

His house was breathtaking. It was so awesome that people were amazed.

Are You Replacing with Your Hands What You Have Lost in Your Soul?

I have learned something about the emotions of God. When we are preoccupied with self, we tend to become neglectful towards the presence of Jesus. When our flesh is having fun, our inner-man is sad. When we feel empty spiritually, we tend to fill our emptiness with empty works. We do all kinds of projects to pacify the emptiness we feel inside! I believe King Solomon had arrived at a place similar to this. Let us read a little more...

The Cat is Out of the Bag!

"But King Solomon loved many foreign women, as well as the daughter of Pharaoh: women of the Moabites, Ammonites, Edomites, Sidonians, and Hittites—from the nations of whom the Lord had said to the children of Israel, 'You shall not intermarry with them, nor they with you. Surely they

will turn away your hearts after their gods.'

"Solomon clung to these in love. And he had seven hundred wives, princesses, and three hundred concubines, and his wives turned away his heart. For it was so, when Solomon was old, that his wives turned his heart after other gods, and his heart was not loyal to the Lord his God, as was the heart of his father David. For Solomon went after Ashtoreth the goddess of the Sidonians, and after Milcom the abomination of the Ammonites. Solomon did evil in the sight of the Lord, and did not fully follow the Lord, as did his father David. Then Solomon built a high place for Chemosh the abomination of Moab, on the hill that is east of Jerusalem, and for Molech the abomination of the people of Ammon. And he did likewise for all his foreign wives, who burned incense and sacrificed to their gods." (1 Kings 11:1-8)

The cat is out of the bag! The Scripture says that King Solomon loved many foreign women, from the nations of whom the Lord had said to the children of Israel, **"You shall not intermarry with them, nor they with you."**

By reading the text, God did not want his people to be involved with foreign women because God understood the power of women. He knew that foreign women worshipped idols and He also knew that men had no control over falling for these pagan women. He knew that King Solomon would end up doing something that would bring him much pain and eventually bring him down!

As the time passed, King Solomon got himself seven-hundred wives and three-hundred concubines. The Scripture says that, **"He clung to these in love."** After King Solomon got older, his wives turned his heart away after other gods, and his heart was not loyal to the Lord his God, as his father David was!

King Solomon finally made altars and worshipped idols himself. The Scripture says, **"Solomon did evil in the sight of the Lord, and did not fully follow the Lord, as did his father David."**

Do you see how this whole thing happened? Can you tell the very place in King Solomon's life where the fire left him? Was it after the anointing came upon him? Was it during the times the world applauded him for his accomplishments? Was it during the building of the temple of the Lord or his own house? When did it happen?

The Kingdom Is Taken Away!

"So the Lord became angry with Solomon, because his heart had turned from the Lord God of Israel, who had appeared to him twice, and had commanded him concerning this thing, that he should not go after other gods, but he did not keep what the Lord had commanded. Therefore the Lord said to Solomon, 'Because you have done this, and have not kept My covenant and My statutes, which I have command-ed you, I will surely tear the kingdom away from you, and give it to your servant. Nevertheless I will not do it in your days, for the sake of your father David; I will tear it out of the hand of your son. However I will not tear away the whole kingdom; I will give one tribe to your son for the sake of my servant David, and for the sake of Jerusalem which I have chosen.'" (1 Kings 11:9-13)

After God speaking to King Solomon twice regarding the matter of his heart going astray, God was angry with King Solomon. This is what God told Solomon: **"Because you have done this, and have not kept My covenant and My statutes, which I have commanded you, I will surely tear the kingdom away from you and give it to your servant."**

Just as God promised King Solomon good fortune if he would walk in all His ways; God also promised "a tearing away" of the kingdom from King Solomon's hands if he did not follow in his direction. He took it all away little by little. Isn't this a tragedy?

King Solomon's Enemies Were Raised by God!

"Now the Lord raised up an adversary against Solomon, Hadad the Edomite; he was a descendant of the king in Edom." (1 Kings 11:14)

"And God raised up another adversary against him, Rezon the son of Eliadah, who had fled from his lord, Hadadezer king of Zobah." (1 Kings 11:23)

"Then Solomon's servant, Jeroboam the son of Nebat, an Ephraimite from Zereda, whose mother's name was Zeruah, a widow, also rebelled against the king." (1 Kings 11:26)

When King Solomon did not turn his heart back to God's will, the Lord unleashed such a fiery trial upon him to bring him back to the place where he had fallen from.

God in His mercy will go after his servants when they have lost their fire. He will not let us to get away so far that He won't come after us and reprimand us and discipline our lives. He does all this because He truly loves us!

The kingdom was eventually taken away from him, and Solomon paid the price for not following the Lord. In all this, we must learn one of the greatest lessons in life: To be always conscious of the Lord's will in our lives, and to make sure that we are always in the center of it!

If the fire starts to die down, it is not because God is running out of the element; if the fire is running low and going out, it is probably because there is no oil in the lamp. If there is no oil in the lamp, it is probably because there is no crushing of olives, no crushing of self in us.

Chapter 10

What in the World Happened to King Uzziah?

"Then all the people of Judah took Uzziah, who was sixteen
years old, and made him king in place of his father Amaziah.
He was the one who rebuilt Elath and restored it to Judah
after Amaziah rested with his ancestors. Uzziah was sixteen
years old when he became king, and he reigned in Jerusalem
fifty-two years. His mother's name was Jekoliah; she was
from Jerusalem. He did what was right in the eyes of the
Lord, just as his father Amaziah had done. He sought God
during the days of Zechariah, who instructed him in the fear
of God. As long as he sought the Lord, God gave him success. He went to war against the Philistines and broke down
the walls of Gath, Jabneh and Ashdod. He then rebuilt towns
near Ashdod and elsewhere among the Philistines. God
helped him against the Philistines and against the Arabs who
lived in Gur Baal and against the Meunites. The Ammonites
brought tribute to Uzziah, and his fame spread as far as the
border of Egypt, because he had become very powerful. Uzziah built towers in Jerusalem at the Corner Gate, at the
Valley Gate, and at the angle of the wall, and he fortified
them. He also built towers in the wilderness and dug many
cisterns, because he had much livestock in the foothills and
in the plain. He had people working his fields, and vineyards
in the hills, and in the fertile lands, for he loved the soil.
Uzziah had a well-trained army, ready to go out by divi-
sions according to their numbers as mustered by Jeiel the
secretary, and Maaseiah the officer, under the direction of
Hananiah, one of the royal officials. The total number of

family leaders over the fighting men was 2,600. Under their command was an army of 307,500 men trained for war, a powerful force to support the king against his enemies. Uzziah provided shields, spears, helmets, coats of armor, bows and slingstones for the entire army. In Jerusalem, he made devices invented for use on the towers and on the corner defenses, so that soldiers could shoot arrows and hurl large stones from the walls. His fame spread far and wide, for he was greatly helped until he became powerful. But after Uzziah became powerful, his pride led to his downfall. He was unfaithful to the Lord his God, and entered the temple of the Lord to burn incense on the altar of incense. Azariah the priest with eighty other courageous priests of the Lord followed him in. They confronted King Uzziah and said, 'It is not right for you, Uzziah, to burn incense to the Lord. That is for the priests, the descendants of Aaron, who have been consecrated to burn incense. Leave the sanctuary, for you have been unfaithful, and you will not be honored by the Lord God.' Uzziah, who had a censer in his hand ready to burn incense, became angry. While he was raging at the priests in their presence before the incense altar in the Lord's temple, leprosy broke out on his forehead. When Azariah the chief priest and all the other priests looked at him, they saw that he had leprosy on his forehead, so they hurried him out. Indeed, he himself was eager to leave, because the Lord had afflicted him. King Uzziah had leprosy until the day he died. He lived in a separate house—leprous, and banned from the temple of the Lord. Jotham his son had charge of the palace and governed the people of the land. The other events of Uzziah's reign, from beginning to end, are recorded by the prophet Isaiah son of Amoz. Uzziah rested with his ancestors and was buried near them in a cemetery that belonged

to the kings, for people said, "He had leprosy." And Jotham his son succeeded him as king." (2 Chronicles 26:1-23)

Successful at Sixteen Years of Age

I want to share a bit of what the Scripture already shows of King Uzziah, and hopefully bring you into this place of greater understanding in God regarding this man's life.

When King Amaziah died, (Uzziah's father) he was chosen to be king of Judah. At the tender age of sixteen, this very young man was anointed to be a leader. People have always wondered if a young individual can lead. The answer is yes!

Uzziah was a restorer and very influential. He reigned in Judah for fifty-two years, and he was not just an ordinary vessel for his day. The Scripture says that, **"He sought God during the days of Zechariah, who instructed him in the fear of God. As long as he sought the Lord, God gave him success."**

Young King Uzziah was not left alone, but somewhere along the line, he was instructed to be a man of prayer. As a matter of fact, the Scripture further verifies that Uzziah was instructed in the fear of the Lord by Zechariah. What a privilege! What a mentor to have in life! The Scripture continues to say that, **"As long as he sought the Lord, God gave him success."**

Is it any wonder that this young man was as powerful as he became? He sought God, and God made him successful. Where have we heard that before? It is all over the Word of God. This is the standard. This is God's way to any form of advancement!

Uzziah: God's Warrior

The Scripture in 2 Chronicles 26:7-15, gives us insight into Uzziah the man of war. He advanced against the Philistines at will, for God was with him. There was nothing that Uzziah couldn't do, for the Lord continued to guide him.

His fame began to spread far and wide. Even the Ammonites began to bring tribute to him, for he became powerful.

"He also built towers in the wilderness and dug many cisterns, because he had much livestock in the foothills and in the plain. He had people working his fields and vineyards in the hills and in the fertile lands, for he loved the soil." Apparently, Uzziah kept growing and growing externally.

His army became extremely powerful and it just seemed that nothing could stop this mighty man of God. There was no doubt in anyone's heart that Uzziah was God's man for the hour; it seemed that everything Uzziah touched would turn to gold.

Little did anyone know that King Uzziah was about to encounter the greatest test of his life. Yes, a test involving his character, commitment, and his true love for God.

After the Power Set In!

"But after Uzziah became powerful, his pride led to his downfall. He was unfaithful to the Lord his God…"

Somewhere in the life of Uzziah, whether he was forewarned by a prophet or the Lord Himself, Uzziah entered into a state of pride. The power which he had attained, became one of his greatest challenges.

My dear friends, isn't this true about anyone who longs to be used by the Lord? A man starts off with humility in his heart and brokenness in his spirit, and by the time he realizes it, this man is now walking in the favor of the Lord. Everything seems to "come easy" as the Lord opens and closes doors for him at his very command. People are praising you and loving you for being so anointed and mightily used of God.

The Scripture continues to say that Uzziah became unfaithful to God. What does this look like? Have you ever given it thought? This is what I believe unfaithfulness unto the Lord looks like: A man who was clothed in humility, started trusting in the Lord after gaining some convincing victories, this man now begins to think that him and God are so close that they have become "buddies." Once you become "buddies" with God, you begin to compare yourself to your buddy, for you think he is your equal. You start thinking that you know a little more than your buddy and lose the respect and honor due to God. Pride does this!

My heart breaks to think of such a thing, as I myself have also had this shameful experience. Thinking that I was someone special and the more the people praised me for my talent and gift, the more I believed it. Then suddenly by the time I knew it, pride had flooded my heart! The next step downward, is one of unfaithfulness to the Lord, and disrespect for all that is godly and divine. How many have reached that point in their lives? Oh, that God would pour mercy on us!

Pride Leads to Lawlessness

"[Uzziah] entered the temple of the Lord to burn incense on the altar of incense. Azariah the priest with eighty other courageous priests of the Lord followed him in. They confronted King Uzziah and said, 'It is not right for you, Uzziah, to burn incense to the Lord. That is for the priests, the descendants of Aaron, who have been consecrated to burn incense. Leave the sanctuary, for you have been unfaithful, and you will not be honored by the Lord God.'

Uzziah, who had a censer in his hand ready to burn incense, became angry. While he was raging at the priests in their presence before the incense altar in the Lord's temple, leprosy broke out on his forehead. When Azariah the chief priest and all the other priests looked at him, they saw that he had leprosy on his forehead, so they hurried him out. Indeed, he himself was eager to leave, because the Lord had afflicted him. King Uzziah had leprosy until the day he died." (2 Chronicles 26:16b-21)

After Uzziah's heart was filled with pride, he felt he could do anything he wanted. A spirit of lawlessness had flooded his life, now and felt he could do whatever his proud heart desired to do. Is there anything more destructive to a man than this?

Uzziah proceeded in this spirit and ventured out to the temple to burn incense unto the Lord. To this, Azariah, the priest, and eighty other courageous priests confronted him for doing this thing that was not right in the sight of the Lord. They told Uzziah that this part of the service unto the Lord was given to the priests, the descendants of Aaron, because they had been consecrated to do the burning of the incense.

Uzziah didn't take this correction lightly and became angry. While he was raging at the priests, leprosy broke out in his forehead! Can you picture this? The Scripture says that Uzziah left the temple in a hurry because the Lord had afflicted him. God have mercy on us!

Eventually, Uzziah died of the leprosy.

Separated, Leprous and Banned!

"He lived in a separate house—leprous and banned from the temple of the Lord." (2 Chronicles 26:21b)

I don't know about you, but when I read the ending of Uzziah, my heart is broken for this man's ending. I am not happy that he ended that way, and so many questions surround my mind as I write this part of my study.

I have counseled many who have been afflicted by separations. Separations in a marriage due to differences in the relationship. The pain of being separated from an individual who once vowed to never leave you and promises made that this particular love was real and that it would last forever.

Separations from a husband or wife by death. When I have spoken to colleagues or friends who have lost their husband or wife because of some lengthy illness or tragic accident—the emotion of being left or abandoned can be so overwhelming, it can send even the most spiritual one, into a tailspin!

Now, the separation from the Lord's divine order, this kind of separation has to be one of the most painful in that it deals with the Eternal One and destiny. To be a sinner without God is one thing, but to be a servant of the Lord and be left without the favor of God upon your life, is totally indescribable! Nothing can measure the ugliness and despair one feels when they have lost the touch of God from their life.

Now, regarding Uzziah—to once having experienced the awesome power of Jehovah upon his life, and to literally see armies fall to his left and to his right by the power of God—and to end separated in a house somewhere, leprous and banned from God's temple, has to be the most painful experience for anyone who had tasted of the Lord's goodness!

Could this have been prevented? Could the fire of God in Uzziah's life been kept burning all the way up to the next generation?

The Fire is Not Automatic!

I believe that a man has to attend to his own fire. A man or woman of God must constantly be in tune with themselves; there must always be a spiritual sensitivity to the Father and to His wishes. One should always walk in check and acknowledge if he is in the faith or not. This too, is part of our calling in God. Here is wisdom: Always tend to the fire!

Chapter 11

Judas Iscariot: The Man Who Never Went into the Fire of God!

"But one of His disciples, Judas Iscariot, Simon's son, who would betray Him, said, 'Why was this fragrant oil not sold for three hundred denarii and given to the poor?'

This he said, not that he cared for the poor, but because he was a thief, and had the money box, and he used to take what was put in it." (John 12:5-6)

As we have been seeing the testimonies of the great men of God in the Old Testament, we cannot but stop and wonder how such anointed and chosen men failed. How did they end up losing all that God had initially promised them and to some large degree, forfeit all that God had intended for them?

It is obvious to me that the fire of the Lord is freely given by God, and at the same time, we are still held responsible to keep the fire burning within our souls. It is our responsibility to get a hold of God and to know what He desires of us!

In meditating upon several examples in the Old Testament of those who lost their fire, I also realized that in the New Testament, several men, servants of Jesus, were also hand-picked for God's service and lost their touch of God, or perhaps the fire of God or simply just never entered fully into what the Lord had intended.

So it doesn't really matter who you are, what time frame you live in, what status you might adhere to, everyone who is chosen of the Lord to burn with holy fire, must also be about the business of cultivating God's fire in his or her heart! This is the task of all of God's servants.

Judas Iscariot, the Treasurer

I want to pick up my study with one particular character, his name, Judas Iscariot.

What do we know about Judas Iscariot? Not a great deal, but enough to form an opinion and perhaps even come to understand why a man who is faulty in their character can abort God's purpose.

When the Lord chooses a man, it is almost like God "taps" him on the shoulder and says to him, "I need you for a particular service in my work."

As we hear God's call, we move forward with holy fear towards all that God wishes (this would be a godly attitude for any servant of Christ). It is God's initial call that sets us apart, but it's our altered responsibility that qualifies us for the purpose!

If we don't make a move towards this spiritual education, we will have a call but with no fire, no passion, no zeal, and no commitment! I believe this is what Judas Iscariot experienced in his short-lived ministry under Christ the Lord.

Hand-Picked by Jesus Himself

One thing is sure about the man Judas Iscariot: (and this can't be debated in my opinion) Jesus chose him! Jesus hand-picked this man to be a servant of His! There is no doubt in anyone's mind that Judas was placed in office by the Lord Himself.

Based on the righteousness of Christ, we know that Jesus made no mistake in choosing Judas Iscariot. As a matter of fact, when God hand-picks any person for any service, He equips them. God will prepare the man through different means for the purpose of training in righteousness. Some face adversity, some face conflicts and temptations of all sorts, and some even encounter failure.

The servant under training will be tested in his character, his emotional equilibrium, his will and in his actions. All these areas will be under probation until God gets His desired result in him. Then comes the release for greater opportunity and fruitfulness.

Now the story begins with Judas Iscariot joining the other disciples, and all of them following Jesus all over Galilee and the surrounding regions. All twelve of His disciples experienced Christ first hand. They all had front row seats! As He preached, as He taught, as He ministered in the power of the Spirit, as He demonstrated compassion, love and mercy, these servants were filled with all kinds of vision and expectations of the kingdom of God. It was like this for a period of about three years. Can one learn something of value in three years? I think it's very possible.

When Will We Learn?

After spending some quality time with the disciples, Jesus begins to challenge them to walk at a higher level. To abandon their lives, hopes, and dreams, and to embrace the Father's will and purpose. To love God with all their heart, mind and soul, was the cry of Jesus towards His twelve disciples.

Judas Iscariot, I'm not sure, but I can only try to understand the man as He walked hand in hand with Jesus and the other disciples—what was he really thinking? Did he actually think that he was going to join the most powerful spiritual force in the universe and walk away with his selfish character intact? I think not. Jesus was going to test this man to the core.

I truly believe that Jesus knew Judas Iscariot very well. He knew Him inside out. I believe that the Lord knew how weak to the flesh this man really was. As the Scripture says in 1 John 2:16, **"For everything in the world—the lust of the flesh, the lust of the eyes, and the pride of life..."** had already made its way into Judas Iscariot's heart.

The Lord loved Judas Iscariot, but Judas Iscariot loved Judas Iscariot way more than anything or anyone!

There might have been a point in Judas' life where a possible change of character could have taken place, but it never really did. I'm sure as He followed Christ day in and day out, there was a burning in his heart. He must have thought to himself, "If I can just get by with showing my face every once in a while, go to the prayer meetings, go from village to village, pretend that I'm into this, then I will collect what is in the money box. I should be alright."

But little did He know that Jesus knew His heart!

Outward Service with No Power!

The Scripture says in John that Judas Iscariot, **"...was a thief, and had the money box, and he used to take what was put in it."**

One could wonder why Jesus being fully aware that this man was a thief, would test him by making him the treasurer. Nothing serves God's purpose more than being tested in the area or areas we covet so much.

When the Lord sent the disciples two by two into the neighboring villages to do signs and wonders, Judas Iscariot was part of that group. He ministered by the word of the Lord. He saw it all and tasted it all. There was no excuse in the life of Judas Iscariot to have ever failed Jesus the Christ.

When the fire of God is released into our heart, we truly are responsible for its upkeep. The Lord can offer His fire and even touch us powerfully with it, but if we don't appropriate ourselves of it, if we don't embrace it, it will never impact us —much less others.

I believe that this was one of Judas' biggest challenges. He wanted the ministry, but not the fire. He wanted the outward blessings but not the inward anointing. One can only go insofar as the power of the flesh and then just die!

One can get close to the fire, but never enter into the fire. This will always mark the difference in the vessel of the Lord. We might want to help out in multiple ways, have desires to see God's kingdom advance powerfully, but yet be without God's eternal flame.

Unless one is touched by God's fire, he himself, will not burn!

It Was All About Self!

Anything that is born of God overcomes the world. Anything that is birthed in the Spirit of the Lord is tainted with God's fingerprints all over! **"Man looks at the outward appearance, but God looks at the heart,"** the Scripture reads.

Jesus could tell the difference. Judas Iscariot wasn't going to fool the Lord Jesus Christ.

As I close this chapter, I want to re-emphasize that in the case of Judas Iscariot, it wasn't that he lost the fire. He simply never had it (at least in my humble opinion.) His interest to follow Jesus was a selfish one. He was looking after his own dreams, plans, ambitions, and future. He was dreaming of how he could "make a name for himself."

In the life of Judas Iscariot, getting all he could from the ministry of the Lord Jesus for selfish reasons was key. In direct comparison, John the Baptist moved by a different spirit. When John the Baptist was asked if he was the Christ, he said no! No way! No how! When asked about him being greater than Christ, he said, **"He must increase but I must decrease."** (John 3:30)

To finish this chapter off, I want to say that just because one has talent, ability, and special God-given giftings —these do not substitute for the fire of God in us! The gift is one thing, the fire is another. Let us make sure that when we minister in His Name, God's fire is accompanying us!

Chapter 12

Demas: The Man Who Deserted God for this Present World!

"Luke the beloved physician and Demas salute you." (Colossians 4:14 AMP)

"And [from] Mark, Aristarchus, Demas, and Luke, my fellow workers." (Philemon 1:24)

"Make every effort to come to me soon. For Demas has deserted me for love of this present world and has gone to Thessalonica…" (2 Timothy 4:9, 10a)

Demas - Touched by Fire!

In reading the different texts above, we can observe that Demas was obviously chosen by Paul to follow in his ministry.

I'm not sure on the different training methods that Paul used for equipping his workers, but without doubt, Demas was a man who at one time had shown positive qualities and great potential.

The Apostle Paul hand-picked this man for service and was well on his way to make a difference in the known world with the gospel of the kingdom.

In studying the different Epistles of Paul, I see that Paul was not, (or at least to me) an easy guy to work for or work with. He had his bouts with John Mark, and some major differences with

Barnabas, but nevertheless, Paul never lowered his standards and expectations of his workers.

The standard was high, and the commitment was without doubt, the key to kingdom work under Paul's direction. Let's just say that not just anyone got the opportunity to join in on the Apostle Paul's apostolic team.

As difficult as it might have been to join Paul's team, Demas made it. He traveled with Paul.

The Lamp Will Be Tested!

As you will discover, reading the Epistles of Paul, you will find many of the challenges this great apostle had to face. There are countless adversities that went on during his career as a servant of Jesus.

From being harassed, to being stoned by Jesus' haters, from shipwrecks to jails —Paul kept the faith through and through. I'm sure there was fears and doubts — but in all of these, Paul was able to navigate and stand by the keeping power of Christ.

I don't believe it was like this for some of his followers; as a matter of fact, Demas happened to be one that didn't quiet "pull through."

In the letter to the Colossians, Demas seems to be one of the leaders spearheading a project by Paul. His name appears along with Luke, the physician on the salutation of the letter. To me this says a lot.

His name being in the forefront of the letter means that Demas was in the "up and up." This man was truly moving with Paul's agenda and getting things done in the kingdom. At least to me it seems that this man was focused and on target to advance the kingdom of God.

I don't doubt that Demas was full of fire during the writing of this letter.

Running Out of Gas?!

When one starts a race, any type of race, an immature runner will usually start very fast and "burn-out" before they even get halfway. This comes because the runner may be lacking experience. On the other hand, an individual who has run races before, understands the need for "pacing" in a race. They don't use all their energy at the start, but rather, they pace themself to conserve energy for the longevity of the race, and with the hope of finishing with great timing. One may even be surprised and take the first-place trophy home!

"And [from] Mark, Aristarchus, Demas, and Luke, my fellow workers." (Philemon 1:24)

When I read this particular verse, here's what I noticed, the name of Demas was dropped on the listing; it went from second place to third place. I don't know if the letter was written like this on purpose, or if Paul could sense that this Christian worker was running out of gas.

Demas was recognized as a worldchanger in the letter to the church in Colosse, but now we find him as one more of the group in Paul's apostolic team. What happened to his status? What is happening to his commitment? What is happening to his fire?

This Present World's Plan

"Make every effort to come to me soon. For Demas has deserted me for love of this present world and has gone to Thessalonica..." (2 Timothy 4:9, 10a)

In the letter to 2 Timothy, which happens to be Paul's last epistle, he mentions quite a bit of information regarding his faith in God and how he trusted God with his whole life. He exhorts Timothy to be a soldier for Jesus and not to mingle with the world.

Paul then reminds Timothy, to work hard at becoming a good worker who is diligent, and to present himself approved by God.

In chapter three of 2 Timothy, Paul warns that in the end times, people would become lovers of themselves, lovers of money, boasters, etc. To all this, Paul tells Timothy to be careful.

Lastly Paul closes his letter with a plea: **"Be diligent to come to me quickly, for Demas has forsaken me, having loved this present world, and has departed...."**

We finally see the big picture of Demas' failure. The man kept fighting until he couldn't overcome the attractions of the world and everything it had to offer. Demas finally left Paul for the world's attraction.

Let us look a little deeper into the part that reads: **"having loved this present world."**

For starters, the world is a corrupt system; it is a corrupt mindset that promotes self-aggrandizing. Demas left the ministry of the Lord for what the world could give him.   Whatever the world offered him then, I bet anything that it didn't satisfy him one bit. Maybe for a season, but not for the long haul. Demas forfeited God's blessing for whatever the world could give him!

Do Not Love the World!

In John 2:15-17, the Scripture reads: **"Do not love the world or the things in the world. If anyone loves the world, the love of the Father is not in him. For all that is in the world—the lust of the flesh, the lust of the eyes, and the pride of life—is not of the Father, but is of the world. And the world is passing away, and the lust of it, but he who does the will of God abides forever."**

The Apostle Paul said that Demas had "forsaken" him for this present world. The fact is that you can't keep the fire of God burning which is internal, while trying to keep the fire of the world, which is external, burning at the same time. It may happen, but not for long!

The Apostle John said, **"Don't love the world or the things in the world. The lust of the flesh, the lust of the eyes, and the pride of life, he adds, is not of the Father but is of the world."**

Any man or woman of God who has been set on fire by God's Spirit is not immune to this type of falling away. This can happen to the most anointed servant of God, as was the case with Demas.

Three things the world uses to turn off the fire in any servant of God:

Lust of the flesh. The lust of the flesh has to do with the old nature, that horrible thing that fights against all that is holy and divine. The flesh, our old nature, has an agenda that pulls opposite to God's plan, desire and purpose. It glories in paralyzing the potential for any kingdom fruit to come forth! It fights and fights to keep God's glory confined to the shell of self.

Lust of the eyes. The lust of the eyes is nothing more and nothing less than what we allow to come in through our eyes. The Bible says that the eyes are the window of the soul. Anything we allow to come in, will bring about consequences. If we allow good things to come inside of us, we will surely bear the fruit of it. In the same way, if we allow anything negative inside our soul, it will also bear its own fruit.

The pride of life. Nothing kills humility faster than the desire to be your own god! The minute you reach the point that you don't need God in your life or His direction, knowledge and/or wisdom, is the minute your life immediately will dry up!

You see, humility is the altar in which God's fire is built upon. Without this altar, God's fire can't be possible! The pride of life to me, is the pursuit of self-aggrandizement. It says, "Be your own god, run your own life!" This too, will be short-lived.

Cultivate, Cultivate, Cultivate!

Demas went after God's will first; he bought into the eternal and impacting will of God. Demas was sold on the idea that God's will would abide forever. He knew better! Yet, in all his understanding of John's words (as written in 1 John 2:15-17), it only touched his mind, but not his heart.

It could have been that his heart had been warmed by God's fire for a season, but as we have been studying, this life must be cultivated. I believe Demas failed in this matter. His fire went out, then his ministry went out —then his whole life went out!

In closing this chapter, when it comes to spiritual matters, one must remember to cultivate every bit of it. What gets you there, will keep you there!

If negligence takes over your life, the old nature will claim its ground by default. Keep cultivating, keep plugging away. There's way too much at stake for you and for those who follow you. Selah.

PART 3

THE APOSTLE PAUL: A MAN OF FIRE!

Lessons on How the Apostle Paul Kept the Fire Burning through a Life of Brokenness.

Chapter 13

Saul of Tarsus: Living a Life of Lifeless Fire!

"Indeed, I myself thought I must do many things contrary to the name of Jesus of Nazareth. This I also did in Jerusalem, and many of the saints I shut up in prison, having received authority from the chief priests, and when they were put to death, I cast my vote against them. And I punished them often in every synagogue and compelled them to blaspheme; and being exceedingly enraged against them, I persecuted them even to foreign cities." (Acts 26:9-11)

When I think of what it means to render service unto the Lord, the words that come to my mind are zeal, passion, and dedication.

I truly believe that without these elements in any endeavor—that endeavor might never get off the ground and accomplish what it was intended to do. I believe you need these three elements for anything you do, if indeed, your goal is to succeed.

It is evident that in the life of Saul of Tarsus, there was something lit; there was evidence that something was instilled at a very young age. It might have come through his mentors, it might have come through his parents, it might have come through his early training under the great Gamaliel.

Whatever the reason behind Saul's passion— it was evident that this man was on fire from a very young age. You can have fire or a passionate fire for many things in life. Saul of Tarsus had it for religion. This is where he started.

Early Life of Saul of Tarsus

Being that we are dealing with the subject in this book of Inextinguishable—I will continue to bring forth this powerful philosophy of life and way of living.

I see this subject matter more of an attitude and way of living than a valiant stand against opposition. To be bold and valiant one time is impressive, but to be of an inextinguishable attitude during a lifespan is admirable and worthy to be imitated.

It is apparent by what we read on Saul of Tarsus that he was a zealous young man. History gives us a brief insight into Saul's life. Let us see…

For starters, we can derive some of Saul's life from the Bible's book of Acts and also his letters as the Apostle Paul to the church communities that he was involved in starting. He is believed to have been born anywhere between 5 BC and 5 AD.

The book of Acts tells us that Saul was also a Roman citizen by birth. He was from a devout Jewish family in the city of Tarsus, one of the largest trading centers in the Mediterranean coast. Tarsus was known for its university not to mention, that Tarsus was also the most influential city in Asia Minor.

Now Paul (Saul) referred himself as being **"of the stock of Israel, of the tribe of Benjamin, a Hebrew of the Hebrews and as touching the law, a Pharisee."**

The Bible says very little of his family or extended family. In Romans 16:7, he states that his relatives, Andronicus and Junia, were Christians before he was, and were prominent among the apostles.

The family had a history of religious piety. Apparently, the family lineage had been very attached to Pharisaic traditions and observances for generations. Acts says that he was in the tent-making profession.

Along with what we know of Saul of Tarsus, we also learn that while he was still very young, he was sent to Jerusalem to receive education at the school of Gamaliel, one of the most noted rabbis in history. The school was noted for giving its students a balanced education, like giving Saul [Paul] a wide exposure to classical literature, philosophy and ethics.

Nothing more is known of Saul's early life until his active part in the stoning of Stephen in Acts 7.

No one will confess more honestly than Saul of his hatred ending in the persecution of Christ's church during his day.

Saul Meets King Jesus!

"But when it pleased God, who separated me from my mother's womb and called me through His grace, to reveal His Son in me, that I might preach Him among the Gentiles..." (Galatians 1:15, 16a)

In Galatians chapter 1, Paul says that God had it all planned out for him. In the timing of God, the Lord revealed himself to Him and called him out to preach. There is no doubt that since birth God had been putting a fire in this young man. It would later prove to be one of his greatest attitudes and tools for planting churches for God.

I believe that God does stuff like this. He will place in our DNA, the qualities that bring about the zeal, the passion and the desire to follow hard after Him. I am amazed at God's planning and timing.

Meanwhile, Saul continued in his attempt to stop, The Way!

By this time in history, Saul's hatred had gone off the wall! He was an intellectual Pharisee, yet with so much anger and on a mission to put away the church of Jesus Christ. Can you imagine that?

Here's Saul's testimony:

"Then Saul, still breathing threats and murder against the disciples of the Lord, went to the high priest and asked letters from him to the synagogues of Damascus, so that if he found any who were of the Way, whether men or women, he might bring them bound to Jerusalem. As he journeyed, he came near Damascus, and suddenly a light shone around him from heaven. Then he fell to the ground, and heard a voice saying to him, 'Saul, Saul, why are you persecuting Me?'
And he said, 'Who are You, Lord?'
Then the Lord said, 'I am Jesus, whom you are persecuting. It is hard for you to kick against the goads.'
So he, trembling and astonished, said, 'Lord, what do You want me to do?'

Then the Lord said to him, 'Arise and go into the city, and you will be told what you must do.'
And the men who journeyed with him stood speechless, hearing a voice but seeing no one. Then Saul arose from the ground, and when his eyes were opened he saw no one. But they led him by the hand and brought him into Damascus. And he was three days without sight, and neither ate nor drank." (Acts 9:1-9)

Forever determined to stop the church of Jesus Christ, Saul finally met the Master! A light came from heaven and stopped Saul cold on his tracks! What an encounter this must have been. The word light means "to shine" of flame. The flame of God consumed the flame of rage in Saul's heart.

My dear friend, what we are: our gifts, talents, and abilities are nothing without the touch of God. We might think that we have it all together—but without the touch of the Master, we are of no eternal good!

Everything we do outside of God's touch will be short-lived; it will leave us broken, disenchanted, empty and longing for reality!

In Saul's case, the light was so powerful, that it knocked him off his horse! It brought him to a new place in life. A place that Saul never thought he would end up.

The touch was so awesome, that Saul was left blind (of selfish vision), bruised (natural ability,gifts, talents, intellectuality), and broken (in heart, selfish dreams).

"Lord, What Do You Want Me to Do?"

These eight words that we read on the heading are the words of a new heart. Something that was not there before, but had just moved in. The attitude to please the Lord in every way possible, had now taken over this bitter heart that Saul had. No one can do this for an individual, only the power of God's fire in the human heart!

You will always know when a man has been altered by God. He will hate everything he used to do and embrace and love everything he used to hate.

Saul of Tarsus had been born-again by the Spirit of God and was well on his way to making history teaming up with God.

The fire of his old nature had been consumed with the fire of God's nature. The proof of this experience in God took Saul to the uttermost parts of the known world to burn brightly for Jesus Christ!

Saul [Paul] is Known in Hell!

"And the evil spirit answered and said, 'Jesus I know, and Paul I know, but who are you?'" (Acts 19:15)

Listen to the evil spirit's testimony of who Saul was to become. The evil spirits knew who Saul (now Paul) was. They could spot him miles away. He was not a Pharisee anymore! He was not trying to be the smartest religious Pharisee anymore! He didn't care about status anymore!

Paul's philosophy now was, **"But what things were gain to me, these I have counted loss for Christ. Yet indeed I also count all things loss for the excellence of the knowledge of Christ Jesus my Lord, for whom I have suffered the loss of all things, and count them as rubbish, that I may gain Christ and be found in Him, not having my own righteousness, which is from the law, but that which is through faith in Christ, the righteousness which is from God by faith; that I may know Him and the power of His resurrection, and the fellowship of His sufferings, being conformed to His death, if, by any means, I may attain to the resurrection from the dead."** (Philippians 3:7-11)

May this be the burning cry within our own hearts as we pursue hard after His heart! Selah.

Chapter 14

The Apostle Paul: A Fire with No Limits!

"…and He died for all, that those who live should live no longer for themselves, but for Him who died for them and rose again." (2 Corinthians 5:15)

God's Initial Fire

When Saul of Tarsus came to the place on the Damascus Road and experienced Jesus's power for the first time in his life, it was as real as it gets!

I am so glad that Saul of Tarsus did not meet a man, a preacher, an evangelist, or an apostle— He met the Man, Christ Jesus in living color. The one who could remove the shame, the guilt, the religion, and fill a wicked and cold heart —all in seconds— met Him face to face.

How a man or woman experiences an encounter with God at first, is very telling of how they will navigate through their Christian faith. When the "real" has come, there is hardly ever room for anything false to take them away from a fiery calling.

Christ Lives in Me

"I have been crucified with Christ; it is no longer I who live, but Christ lives in me, and the life which I now live in the flesh, I live by faith in the Son of God, who loved me and gave Himself for me. I do not set aside the grace of God, for

if righteousness comes through the law, then Christ died in vain." (Galatians 2:20)

It is apparent that by the time Paul wrote these powerful words in the book of Galatians, Paul was already experiencing first hand revelations of God's plan and the purpose for God's church. The fire that was in Christ was now upon Paul's life.

Paul understood that His life was nothing without the living Christ. He also knew that Jesus Christ was now living inside of him and leading him to do exploits. Paul was totally a God-possessed man!

Representing Christ as an ambassador was now going to be Paul's life. He would now begin an empire-building project for God. Just as Christ moved upon the earth where He was rejected, Paul would move upon the earth with the anointing God had given him.

An Apostle of Jesus!

"Paul, an apostle of Christ Jesus through the will of God, according to the promise of the life which is in Christ Jesus." (2 Timothy 1:1)

The fire of God burned brightly in Paul's life, bringing him into many geographical places. With the touch of God upon his life, Paul recognized that God had hand-picked him for the work of an apostle. Training workers, planting churches, and preaching the gospel of the kingdom of God, was what Paul was into in his walk with God.

One of the things that I have seen in a man who has fire—is the way that he or she leads. They have a certainty about them, a confidence that is so powerful, that nothing will deter them. Paul was of such status.

When you know what God wants from you; when you realize the reason of why you were created …this emotion alone, will take you to places you never imagined.

The fire of God is the need of the hour. Not more ideas, not more arguments on theological perspectives, no more apologetics, but a true fire come from heaven— this and only this, can get a man or woman to the place where he needs to be with God.

That I May Know Him!

Obviously, the fire inside Paul's heart burned so bright and so deep that it made him be what he became —a true servant that could be trusted.

Though Paul did great deeds and accomplished powerful thing in the name of Jesus, he was not going to stop there; the fire in him was burning for so much more!

Listen to his wish and prayer as he unfolds it in his letter to the Philippians: **"…that I may know Him and the power of His resurrection, and the fellowship of His sufferings, being conformed to His death, if, by any means, I may attain to the resurrection from the dead."** (Philippians 3:10-11)

Paul wanted to experience the fullness of all that God had prepared for him in this life. He was not going to live his life with regrets, retreats, or reserves! No sir. Paul was determined to go the extra mile and said, **"That I may know Him!"**

Paul wanted to know Jesus in deeper ways! This should be the desire of every born-again believer.

Secular Fire vs God's Fire

"If anyone else thinks he may have confidence in the flesh, I more so: circumcised the eighth day, of the stock of Israel, of the tribe of Benjamin, a Hebrew of the Hebrews; concerning the law, a Pharisee; concerning zeal, persecuting the church; concerning the righteousness which is in the law, blameless, But what things were gain to me, these I have counted loss for Christ. Yet indeed I also count all things loss for the excellence of the knowledge of Christ Jesus my Lord, for whom I have suffered the loss of all things, and count them as rubbish, that I may gain Christ." (Philippians 3:4-8)

What once was illusive to Saul of Tarsus; what once gave Saul of Tarsus dignity, human acceptance and status; what gave him position among the great Pharisaic movement, all the accolades and all the pomp—no longer had a hold on him. The fire of God had come and devoured all the works of the flesh! Do you see why we need the fire of God to burn in us?

Paul adds in his letter, **"But what things were gain to me, these I have counted loss for Christ."**

What is Paul saying here? He is saying that all his trophies and all his earthly dreams— all of it —no longer mattered. All these wonderful accomplishments which by earthly standards were important at one time, had no hold on him now. Paul was so full of fire, that the flesh had been burned off!

Why is it that not many are able to break free from a popular crowd? A promising contract? An opportunity to get further recognized for an accomplishment? Because there is no godly fire in sight!

Left for Dead!

"Then Jews from Antioch and Iconium came there; and having persuaded the multitudes, they stoned Paul and dragged him out of the city, supposing him to be dead. However, when the disciples gathered around him, he rose up and went into the city. And the next day he departed with Barnabas to Derbe." (Acts 14:19-21)

Now the fire of God will take you into places where those who don't have fire will not go. This is a fact. The fire of God doesn't see limitations; human emotion and enthusiasm is always second-guessing itself.

Paul preached with holy zeal and holy fire. Finally, some Jews couldn't take it any longer and they persuaded the multitudes against Paul and stoned him and dragged him out of the city, supposing they had killed him. I'm telling you, unless the fire of God is burning inside of you brightly, you will not make it!

It was here where we don't really know if Paul really died or not, but enough to say that after praying for him, Paul got up again and went back into the city. He went to continue the task he was set to do. It's the fire of God that will do this in you.

Today many leaders quit. They give-up because they got beaten up by the enemy. Why do people give up easily? There is no fire! Wonder no more…if there is no fire, there is no desire!

One would have thought and said to Paul, "Paul, you need to slow down – you almost got killed the other day!" Paul turned a deaf ear and continued to move with holy fire.

Dying for Jesus' Sake!

"Now when we heard these things, both we and those from that place pleaded with him not to go up to Jerusalem. Then Paul answered, 'What do you mean by weeping and breaking my heart? For I am ready not only to be bound, but also to die at Jerusalem for the name of the Lord Jesus.'

So when he would not be persuaded, we ceased, saying, 'The will of the Lord be done.'" (Acts 21:12-14)

One of the most intriguing passages I have read regarding the Apostle Paul was this one above.

In the Book of Acts, the brothers are trying to encourage Paul to not visit Jerusalem, that it wouldn't be a good idea—being that he was "wanted," and that misfortune might follow him there.

But Paul was not moved one bit. He never flinched at their words but instead insisted all the more. Here is an instance where fire overpowers emotion! The will of God overpowers the will of self! Paul said, **"What do you mean by weeping and breaking**

my heart? For I am ready not only to be bound, but also to die at Jerusalem for the name of the Lord Jesus."
I wonder how many people would submit to this type of life? How many would succumb to the popular vote? How many would actually pull through and do the will of the Lord, even when it seems dangerous and inconvenient?

The fire of God will undoubtedly consume all flesh and put things into perspective for anyone who allows it to do so! Invite His fire.

Chapter 15

Secrets Behind a Man of Fire!

"But I want you to know, brethren, that the things which happened to me have actually turned out for the furtherance of the gospel, so that it has become evident to the whole palace guard, and to all the rest, that my chains are in Christ; and most of the brethren in the Lord, having become confident by my chains, are much more bold to speak the word without fear." (Philippians 1:12-14)

While studying and meditating over the life of the Apostle Paul, I can't help but notice the intensity that clothed this great servant of Christ. His life was a blazing ball of eternal fire!

After dealing with some afflictions earlier in his endeavor to touch lives for Christ among the Jews and Gentiles, Paul was no less motivated and no less perseverant for the cause of Christ! This alone is an amazing thought.

In today's Christianity —all too often, believers bail out from serving God. The reasons are not even good excuses. People get offended by another Christian, others get upset, and some just can't get over their personal struggles with sin and compromise, disqualifying themselves altogether.

In Chains

In his letter to the Philippians, the Apostle Paul writes about his experience of being in jail. Though things looked grim for those looking from the outside in, Paul was filled with excitement and the great opportunity to preach the gospel and extend it, in spite of being in such state.

In Philippians 1:19-21: **"For I know that this will turn out for my deliverance through your prayer and the supply of the Spirit of Jesus Christ, according to my earnest expectation and hope that in nothing I shall be ashamed, but with all boldness, as always, so now also Christ will be magnified in my body, whether by life or by death. For to me, to live is Christ, and to die is gain."**

A man or woman of fire is hardly ever thinking of themselves. As a matter of fact, Paul was talking about magnifying Christ in his body, whether by life or by death. Obviously, the conditions were adverse, but Paul's heart condition was set on glorifying Christ in whatever manner he found himself - whether living or dying.

In essence Paul was saying, "I'm not going to lose on the deal! If I live, I get Christ; If I die, I gain more of Christ!" What made Paul think this way? The fire of God in him!

Rejoice!

"Rejoice in the Lord always. Again I will say, rejoice! Let your gentleness be known to all men. The Lord is at hand. Be anxious for nothing, but in everything by prayer and supplication, with thanksgiving, let your requests be made known to God; and the peace of God, which surpasses all understanding, will guard your hearts and minds through Christ Jesus." (Philippians 4:4-7)

As Paul sits in the jail, he begins to write letters of comfort and assurance to God's servants outside. A heart that is set on fire by God, does not see opposition as something to be focused upon. Paul is burning with holy zeal and will not be quieted!

He could have felt sorry for himself inside the jail. He could have complained to God regarding his present state. He could have blamed God for this or that! But No! He saw it all as God's way of extending His glory through him on the earth. Glory to King Jesus

He continues to say, **"Be anxious for nothing, but in every-thing by prayer."** How powerful is the condition of Paul's heart? How profound is Paul's revelation of the greatness of Christ in him? How intense if God's fire in him?

In Afflictions

"Are they Hebrews? So am I. Are they Israelites? So am I. Are they the seed of Abraham? So am I. Are they ministers of Christ?—I speak as a fool—I am more: in labors more abun-dant, in stripes above measure, in prisons more frequently, in deaths often. From the Jews five times I received forty stripes minus one. Three times I was beaten with rods; once I was stoned; three times I was shipwrecked; a night and a day I have been in the deep; in journeys often, in perils of waters, in perils of robbers, in perils of my own countrymen, in perils of the Gentiles, in perils in the city, in perils in the wilderness, in perils in the sea, in perils among false breth-ren; in weariness and toil, in sleeplessness often, in hunger and thirst, in fastings often, in cold and nakedness—besides the other things, what comes upon me daily: my deep con-

cern for all the churches. **In Damascus the governor, under Aretas the king, was guarding the city of the Damascenes with a garrison, desiring to arrest me; but I was let down in a basket through a window in the wall, and escaped from his hands. It is doubtless not profitable for me to boast. I will come to visions and revelations of the Lord: I know a man in Christ who fourteen years ago—whether in the body I do not know, or whether out of the body I do not know, God knows—such a one was caught up to the third heaven. And I know such a man—whether in the body or out of the body I do not know, God knows—how he was caught up into Paradise and heard inexpressible words, which it is not lawful for a man to utter. Of such a one I will boast; yet of myself I will not boast, except in my infirmities. For though I might desire to boast, I will not be a fool; for I will speak the truth. But I refrain, lest anyone should think of me above what he sees me to be or hears from me. And lest I should be exalted above measure by the abundance of the revelations, a thorn in the flesh was given to me, a messenger of Satan to buffet me, lest I be exalted above measure. Concerning this thing I pleaded with the Lord three times that it might depart from me. And He said to me, "My grace is sufficient for you, for My strength is made perfect in weakness." Therefore most gladly I will rather boast in my infirmities, that the power of Christ may rest upon me. Therefore I take pleasure in infirmities, in reproaches, in needs, in persecutions, in distresses, for Christ's sake. For when I am weak, then I am strong."** (2 Corinthians 11:22-28; 11:32-12:11)

What is Behind a Man of Fire?

I remember my spiritual mentor many years ago telling me, "David, there is reason why God uses certain men! It was not for their degrees in theology or divinity. It wasn't for their talent. It was not for their giftings. It was for their brokenness!"

After being impacted by such words, I then started to realize that my mentor's statement was so true; every biography that I had read was filled with paragraphs and full pages of suffering, pain, and misery. The testimonies were filled with songs of deliverance and how the Lord sustained them over and over in their mission endeavor. All these workers for God understood with Job when he said,

"Look, I go forward, but He is not there,
And backward, but I cannot perceive Him;
When He works on the left hand, I cannot behold Him;
When He turns to the right hand, I cannot see Him.
But He knows the way that I take;
When He has tested me, I shall come forth as gold."
(Job 23:8-10)

When my mentor sent me to pioneer my first church, he said to me, "David— God always makes a way for a man of prayer!"

I am glad I listened to that wise piece of counsel!

The Apostle Paul was indeed a broken vessel for God. He had experienced just about everything under the sun in his pursuit to establish God's house on the earth. He faced much adversity, but God was faithful over and over to Paul. God will always keep His word to his servants of fire!

God told Paul, **"My grace is sufficient for you, for My grace is made perfect in weakness!"**

A Crown of Righteousness Awaits!

"For I am already being poured out as a drink offering, and the time of my departure is at hand. I have fought the good fight, I have finished the race, I have kept the faith. Finally, there is laid up for me the crown of righteousness, which the Lord, the righteous Judge, will give to me on that Day, and not to me only but also to all who have loved His appearing." (2 Timothy 4:6-8)

After running with God's will and God's fire upon His heart for years, Paul finishes up His writings by saying and testifying that he had fought the good fight— that he had finished the race and had kept the faith. He proceeded to say that a crown of righteousness had now been laid up for him which the Lord Jesus had promised. What a man of God, what a man of fire.

- **The fire will take you through your adversity!**

As I close this particular chapter, I want to say that God's fire is reserved for those who are serious about "burning out" for God! Those who see the test and trials of life as opportunity for growth, revelation, and deeper brokenness.

- **The fire will help you fight the good fight!**

When one gets weary of the fight, when one feels like quitting his or her outreach to the lost because of unfavorable circumstances, when one believes that his time on earth is done because of discouragement—the let me tell you, the fire of God will take you through the fight! It is God's fire that will empower you and overshadow you to conquer. Get full of God's fire!

- **The fire will help you finish your race!**

How you start a race is not as important as how you finish it. We can all get head starts in life, but not everybody always ends or finishes well. Too many quit too early! Too many are knocked off by the devil's lies and schemes, but those who endure till the end, will reap their reward.

Chapter 16

"Let Me Burn Out for God!"

"Let me burn out for God. After all, whatever God may appoint, prayer is the great thing. Oh, that I may be a man of prayer!"

-Henry Martyn (1781-1812)

Reading some of the notes from the great servant of God, Henry Martyn, my heart is re-awakened with the desire and the passion to be a man of fire. I can't say that I have attained such a level, but as my mentor used to say, "I'm working at it!"

Blinded by Fire!

As I have been contemplating the completion of this manuscript— thinking and meditating on how I wanted to close this last chapter, I was taken back to my early beginnings as a hungry, zealous, and passionate man, who had nothing but God, and who wanted nothing but God.

It was these emotions, coupled with God's anointing and faith that have caused me to cross bridges, take steps into the unknown, hang in there when it was more convenient not to do so, and continue knocking until some type of door would open for me.

At first, I thought I had lost my mind when I left my job to follow Jesus. I remember hearing this particular hymn for the first time - it totally revolutionized me and set my course on an unending path of fire:

Hear the Lord of harvest sweetly calling,
"Who will go and work for Me today?
Who will bring to Me the lost and dying?
Who will point them to the narrow way?"

Speak, my Lord, speak, my Lord,
Speak, and I'll be quick to answer Thee;
Speak, my Lord, speak, my Lord,
Speak, and I will answer, "Lord, send me."

When the coal of fire touched the prophet,
Making him as pure, as pure can be,
When the voice of God said, "Who'll go for us?"
Then he answered, "Here I am, send me."

Millions now in sin and shame are dying,
Listen to their sad and bitter cry;
Hasten, brother, hasten to the rescue;
Quickly answer, "Master, here am I."

Soon the time for reaping will be over;
Soon we'll gather for the harvest home;
May the Lord of harvest smile upon us,
May we hear His blessed, "Child, well done."

- George Bennard (1873-1958)

From the day that I heard such fervent and passionate heart —
my own heart never turned back for anything less. It almost

seemed like the fire blinded me from looking back! All fear was gone; all insecurity taken away; all doubt erased— nothing of that was left, nothing but a burning fire to do what pleased the Father!

Crossroads in the Walk of Fire!

Anyone who decides to follow Jesus wholeheartedly, knows that a life of surrender must precede it. You can't follow Jesus and also have it "your way." That will lead to a big conflict in your soul and spirit.

Walking with Jesus is filled with crossroads. Yes, there are those spiritual "forks" in the road when you must choose one way or the other. This will not only happen once, but often.

There will be countless times that you and I will be challenged to take uncomfortable steps of faith.

If you have been walking with God for some time, you know very well that you cannot see God's way with natural vision. It takes spiritual vision to discern and follow God's direction. The Prophet Isaiah said, **"And your ears will hear a word behind you, "This is the way, walk in it," whenever you turn to the right or to the left."** (Isaiah 30:21)

We can rest assured that if we go after God's heart, He will always lead us in the best way— always!

As the fire of God leads us into unknown places (whether spiritual or geographical), one must not quench the fire of God. It is the fire of God that goes before us and burns up all His enemies;

we have nothing to fear if we stay within the sphere of His fire.

When Fire Tests Your Faith!

It wasn't long after that I had entered full time ministry that the testing began. I had really enjoyed the "honeymoon" period, but I just didn't think my "honeymoon" would be that short!

After praying for months for our ministry to grow and increase financially, nothing happened. The bills were piling up, and the AC broke down. The summer time in our region is extremely hot (actually one of my friends said, 'You can actually see hell from the church's rooftop!') So, imagine being in a cylinder-block building with no windows at 105 degree heat and trying to sing and preach with no ventilation.

It was during this time that things got really hard and then things just got worse and worse.

One day I got home from an exhausting day of testing and nothing to look forward to, when I seriously thought, "'What mistake have I done in leaving my good paying job?' What was I thinking?"

On this very day, I checked my mailbox and to my surprise, someone had sent me a letter which was folded in three parts. Inside of the letter was a word of encouragement along with an excerpt from George Mueller's autobiography. Also, with my letter was a $5 bill.

As I opened the letter and started reading the words in it, I was warned by the writer to not go to "Egypt" for help, but to trust the One who had called me into the ministry. The letter went on to say that God would sustain me and keep me at all times. To remain faithful and to trust God with my life and ministry. Up to today, I still have never found out who sent me that letter.

I was so broken by the personal letter and the excerpt from George Mueller's life. I must also add that this was one of the most powerful encounters with God that helped me align my whole ministry and to continue seeking for more of God's fire in my life!

Why the Title, Inextinguishable!?

I divided this manuscript into three parts as you have already read: *Created for Burning, Where Did the Fire Go? and The Apostle Paul: A Man of Fire!*

As I meditated upon the Lord's heart for this message, I felt the Spirit of God saying to me, "Share all I have done in you. Make mention of how it all began. Talk about the fire that I have instilled in you and how it has taken you to various places."

Also, the Lord told me to write about the various Bible characters who experienced the fire but then lost it! This was a challenging part— being that we have all been at the place of testing hanging by a thread of grace.

To finish off this book, God told me to speak of the great Apostle Paul. His life as a Pharisee, His life as a follower of Jesus, and his countless furnaces of trial and pain.

To sum it all up: God said, "David, Paul went through much

adversity —yet, he never burned-off, burned-out, or quit on me! You can do the same. Live an inextinguishable life —just like my servant Paul.

My Prayer for You!

My prayer is that your heart will be touched, moved, and challenged for more of God's fire in your own life. That has been my heart-cry since the day God touched me; it continues to be my heart's desire and passion —not only for myself, but for everything I do for Jesus!

May your heart burn for more of Him until all of you is engulfed in His holy fire; then say with great conviction just like Henry Martyn, *"Let me burn out for God!"*

Ministry Information

For more information regarding the ministry of Masterbuilder Ministries, feel free to email us at:

mayorga1126@gmail.com

Also, feel free to check out our website at:
www.masterbuildertx.com

For more books written by David Mayorga, please see our online bookstore at:

www.shabarpublications.com